PORCELAIN
THE ELITE OF CERAMICS

PORCELAIN
THE ELITE OF CERAMICS

MOLDS AND THEIR USES
TECHNIQUES • COLORING METHODS
CREATING YOUR OWN PORCELAIN HEIRLOOMS

RONALD SERFASS

CROWN PUBLISHERS, INC., NEW YORK

*To Pam, Rick, and
Dushél*

Designed by Ruth Kolbert Smerechniak

*Printed in the United States of America
Published simultaneously in Canada by
General Publishing Company Limited*

Library of Congress Cataloging in Publication Data

·Serfass, Ronald, 1949-
    Porcelain—the elite of ceramics.

    Includes index.
    1. Pottery craft.   I. Title.
TT920.S43   1979   738.1'4   79-12805
ISBN 0-517-53621-8
ISBN 0-517-53623-4 pbk.

CONTENTS

CONTENTS

2

PORCELAIN TECHNIQUES
51

3

COLORING
91

4

CREATING YOUR OWN
PORCELAIN HEIRLOOMS
117

CONTENTS

ACKNOWLEDGMENTS

Many generous manufacturers and companies have allowed me to include their names in this book. Without their approval I would never have been able to put this book together. Their names and supply information can be found in the back of the book.

Thanks are also extended to Mildred Berger, who had sufficient confidence in my work to set up an interview with the famed Boehm studio of Trenton, New Jersey. It was she who really got me working toward this fine art, at which I now make my living.

I would also like to mention Ann, Willow, June, and Helen from Staaten Ceramics of Staten Island, New York, whom I taught in classes while I was writing the book. The dues they paid me for teaching them helped me through the months of writing and working. My deepest gratitude to Isabel Dahl, who also believed in my work enough to help me out financially in my business ventures.

Many fine stores and jewelers who have sold my work through the past few years have also had enough confidence in it to allow it to be displayed with many other fine porcelains from throughout the world. I express my deepest thanks to Musselmans Jewelers, of Easton, Bethlehem, and Quakertown, Pennsylvania; Hamilton Jewelers of Trenton, New Jersey; Bailey, Banks, and Biddle of Philadelphia; Appel Jewelers of Allentown, Pennsylvania; Limited Editions of East Windsor, New Jersey; The Gift Shop of Tulsa, Oklahoma; Designers Choice of Pompano Beach, Florida; and Rhodes Gift Shop in my hometown of Newtown, Pennsylvania.

Thanks to my brother and sister-in-law, Dwayne and Twosie, who assisted me with security for a private studio gallery, the Dushél Galleries, on 94 Bustleton Pike, Churchville, Pennsylvania 18966.

I would like to mention my cousin Joyce Butz, who gave me business help throughout the last few months. And I would also like to thank those studios and ceramic shops that allowed me to come to teach in their shops in order that I might demonstrate and spread abroad the porcelain techniques so greatly wanted.

Most thankful I am to my parents, who have allowed me to use up half their basement to create and further my endeavors in the porcelain field.

China-painting class taught by Ronald Serfass.

PREFACE

To many, porcelain is one of the finest collectible items in the art world. To this day pieces bought for hundreds of dollars are valued and sold for thousands, merely because of the quantity manufactured, the time of manufacturing, and the ornateness of the specific creation.

To the avid collector porcelain is an investment with the prospect in later years of getting much more for the piece than was paid for it. And in most cases, this is what happens.

But what about the porcelain lover who cannot afford the prices quoted by many of the porcelain galleries and fine jewelers? Where are they to purchase the beautiful works of art produced in porcelain?

My answer is to learn to create it yourself. Yes. Having formerly worked in the finest porcelain studio in the world, decorating and doing china painting, I realized that the same artwork could be done outside a major studio. But the teaching of this art is quite unavailable. Too many times someone who knows about porcelain will not give you all the information you need to know to create your own objects.

Knowing what I went through to find information, I am proud to be able to relay any information I can to anyone who wants to learn this fine art.

I have to admit, the experience of working for the porcelain studio was priceless, but there I learned only the decorating techniques of china painting. So the rest of the art I had to learn through trial and error until I finally realized what porcelain really allowed me to do with it. I must tell you I made a lot of errors until I learned what I needed to know. There were times when, having fired a beautiful creation, the whole piece came out sagged out of shape. I propped it with porcelain props, but if they fell out while firing, the extending piece would just fall and sag. Then I learned of a ceramic fiber used at the porcelain studios where I worked. I tried it and it worked miracles. I very seldom have any problems now.

I can remember once when I was in a hurry to see what a piece would look like when fired I put the piece into the kiln wet and fired it too fast. It exploded all over the kiln, and what a mess it was! Thank goodness I didn't have the kiln filled, or the whole kiln load of pieces would have been damaged.

This book is for anyone who wants to learn all about molds, pouring, porcelain slip, how to fire your kilns, creative techniques used with porcelain, flowers, lace draping, birds, and the technique of china painting. I put into it everything I could think of that would convey the information needed to create in porcelain.

Having taught many classes in porcelain creating and china painting, I know how many ceramists are eager to learn. Most of them told me they were unable to find anyone qualified to teach it thoroughly. So, having heard this complaint so often, I knew there had to be some way to get to all these people.

That is why I wrote this book, *Porcelain: The Elite of Ceramics*. The way I have arranged its contents should help readers to understand the processes more easily. I have divided it into four different chapters. Chapter one deals with all the technical information needed to follow porcelain techniques and china painting. The second chapter is on techniques in porcelain, the third is on coloring and glazes, and the fourth is on special creative projects, including an elaborate bird creation.

If you read this book all the way through before starting to work on your projects, you will avoid many pitfalls. All projects can be related back to the first chapter, where the know-how information is covered.

I hope you enjoy using this book as much as I enjoyed putting it together.

1

RULES AND PREPARATIONS FOR PORCELAIN CREATING

PREPARING ONESELF

There are three important factors in preparing oneself for the fine art of porcelain creating: patience, quality, and perfection.

Many ceramic studios and hobbyists have ignored the first principle completely, and thus have done a disservice to this medium, concluding that problems arising in porcelain aren't worth the time and effort. But problems occur only out of ignorance, and ignorance leads to failure. Don't let these attitudes deprive you of creative enjoyment and pleasure. Start thinking creatively, suppressing those taboos and worries that have plagued your mind. Discipline yourself and learn to put the true art of porcelain in its proper perspective. At times you will feel like smashing the whole project, but that is when discipline and patience are needed.

Another factor important in preparation is consciousness of quality.

To develop this you must search for the finest materials and learn to use them wisely. With all the products on the market, many will not be suitable. Depending on the availability of material, you may have to test and retest till you find the one product best suited to your purpose. Tools and miscellaneous items listed throughout the book can be obtained at most ceramic shops. However, a few porcelain products will have to be purchased from the manufacturers themselves.

Perfection, the most important factor of all, is in the hands and mind of the artist and can only be brought out through many hours of painstaking work and experimenting.

Upon studying the rules and preparations in this chapter you will begin to understand the properties, flexibilities, and unique possibilities of this medium. As you progress, step-by-step procedures will allow perfection to gradually become a habit throughout all your work.

Remember that problems may arise during your artistic adventures, but they will lead to better understanding of the medium.

THE MOLD

PURPOSE OF THE MOLD

The mold is a negative impression of the positive-shaped sculpting made out of plaster. Sometimes a bit of hydrastone is also added to the plaster mix, making the mold a bit harder, giving it a longer life.

When the slip is poured into the mold, the recessed impression inside creates a duplicate of the original sculpting from which the mold was made. Without the use of a mold, one would have to re-create each individual piece by hand.

Everything imaginable can be bought in mold company lines, such as dishes, lamps, ashtrays, animals, birds, and even special event and holiday items. New designs in molds are being developed every day by major companies. Many of them produce molds from your own sculpting, and ornaments if needed.

MOLD MAKING

Mold making is an art in itself. Many steps are taken in the process, so many that it can take days, depending on how elaborate the sculptured piece is.

The KOALA BEAR, one of my original creations, took the mold maker a few weeks to complete. It took nineteen dissections to be able to make the molds needed for re-creation. The number of molds made to pour and cast the pieces came to twelve. They included the bear's body, arms, and legs, the leaves, flowers, and branches, and the base.

(14)

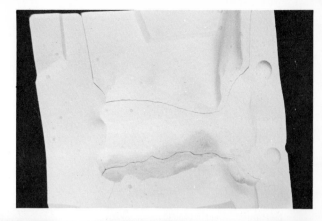

A mold has a negative impression inside that creates the positive shape that is the casting in porcelain. You can see the lines that are the joining of the mold parts.

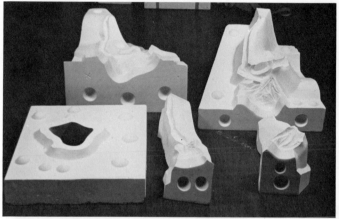

The mold for the base of KOALA BEAR, an original piece that I produced under my business name, Dushél, has five mold parts to band together to pour one piece in the construction of the creation. All molds have at least two parts, depending on how extensive the creation is.

These are the twelve molds that had to be made to cast all the pieces dissected from the koala bear creation.

Many mold parts must be banded together to cast the many pieces for assembling. You can see how extensive it is in making a mold when an ornate object must be reproduced.

KOALA BEAR

Ronald Serfass. Limited edition by Dushél Porcelain Studio. After assemblage and firing, the piece was china painted.

Detail quality of the molds is essential to pour sharply detailed pieces such as these. These are cast from one mold, with no stick-ons.

The kingfisher on the right was porcelain high-fired to bisque; the one on the left is greenware unfired. You can see the shrinkage that occurs during a firing.

In order to create the three-dimensional object, these cuts were needed. Otherwise all the undercuts would need to be filled in, making the piece flat and unattractive.

After the dissection, a waste mold is made from plaster. The plaster is applied all over the clay section. Then the plaster is removed carefully so the clay model can be removed.

This waste mold has the negative impression of the sculpting. Plaster is poured into this waste mold to form a plaster cast of the clay model. Then the waste mold is discarded, and that is how the waste mold got its name.

After the plaster cast is removed, the fine detail is sculpted into the plaster cast. When all the fine work is done to the plaster pieces, a block mold is made from each plaster cast. This new mold is the mold that is slip-cast to re-create the pieces for assembling for production.

From the block mold, case molds are made. These are the ones used to cast new block molds for production casting. The case mold is made from hydrastone, since there is usually only one made. And hydrastone is a hard substance that will outlast any plaster mold. Without this case mold there would be no way to reproduce new molds for casting.

After the block molds are poured you can pour all the pieces you

(17)

want without worrying about breaking a mold. You always have the case mold from which to make new ones.

It all seems quite complicated, and I know it really is. It is much easier to have a master mold maker do it for you if you really have something unique to produce.

The mess and time involved in mold making are unbelievable. It really is a whole craft in itself. Molds need to be tight so seam lines don't show up; if they do, there is a great deal of extra and time-consuming work involved in production.

Good luck to you who would like to make your own molds. But I feel my time as an artist is more valuable. I'd rather leave the mold making to the mold maker.

TYPES OF MOLDS

For the novice who is really interested in learning to pour his own porcelain greenware, there are student molds. These molds are usually in two pieces, small and not too cumbersome to learn with. They are also less expensive. But they are the same as other molds except for their size.

Two-piece molds are by far the best to start with, especially if you haven't done any pouring before. Many beautifully shaped vases, bells, dishes, and small ornaments can be found in this category of mold, and many are as detailed as the larger ones.

There are also molds that consist of as many as four or more parts. These are needed because of the extending areas and deep undercuts on the sculptured object. Any arms, legs, wings on birds, branches on trees, or any protruding parts need separate mold sections. Without them, when the mold is opened the casting would pull apart where the undercuts would grab the mold cavities.

If an object has many extending parts and undercuts, these parts need to be dissected from the main structure. These cut-off pieces also need molds made of them, thus causing a number of extra molds to be poured. These are called stick-ons, which then are assembled on the main object.

Ornate creations such as birds and animal wildlife take as many as nine or more molds to pour, all the pieces needing assemblage afterward. These molds usually cost more than a hundred dollars if bought from a mold company. Custom-made molds made especially for you can cost as much as a thousand or more dollars, depending on the number of molds needed to be made.

If you know exactly where you are headed in your porcelain endeavors, you will know which molds you want and how much money you wish to spend. Remember that every time you sell a piece of greenware, bisque, or a creation, you are making your money back plus a profit, after the cost of the mold is covered.

CONDITION OF MOLD

When buying a mold make sure the company has a reputation for making good molds. Some molds have pit marks when you buy them; others will develop them after you have poured them a few times. The pit marks appear when cheap plaster is used, and bubbles get trapped in the mold when the plaster is poured.

Some molds will lose their detail very quickly when they have been poured a few times. This is also caused by using a low grade of plaster. Hydrastone added will give the mold a longer life, but not all companies use it.

Mold companies are always pouring new molds, and when you buy them they are usually wet. That's fine. It will keep them from chipping and cracking while you are transporting them to your home. But a wet mold cannot usually be poured. The wetness of the mold will not let the liquid slip build up enough to create the thickness needed for casting. So you have to wait about a week or two, depending on the size of the mold, for it to dry and be usable.

There are some mold companies that dry molds ahead of time for you if you order ahead. It is a convenience, especially when you want to take a mold home to pour right away.

All molds you buy should be taped straight and tight so that, when drying, they will not warp. All mold companies do this. But once in a while a mold will have a mind of its own, becoming warped and loose. If this happens, the locks and joints on the mold will not tighten and the slip will seep through the loose seams, making large seam lines on the poured greenware. More cleaning will be needed later on, so make sure the mold is tight-fitting and has no loose seam lines inside.

Detail quality is essential if you are to create beautifully finished porcelain. All detail should be clear and sharp or it is useless even to begin.

Some companies use their master molds for pouring out molds so many times that their detail is lost, thus passing onto us poor detailed molds for casting.

The only way you can be sure of detail is to open each and every mold you buy. Never buy a mold that is worn, because if a mold company gets away with that it will do it all the time. So be picky and remember that lost detail will make a beautiful piece plain and drab. You want to see the mold inside and out. If it is not to your liking, refuse it and ask for another. If not, look for another design. Don't sacrifice detail to indulge your hankering for a specific design.

SHAPE OF OBJECT

The shape of the object that is to be poured is important. Some things will fire well in porcelain, others will not.

A vase, for instance, with a narrow-rimmed bottom probably would not hold up to the extreme heat around the bottom narrow rim. The stress of weight from the top would make the small narrow area unstable and cause the top to sag or collapse.

Heat causes porcelain to become soft, and, when shrinking, it moves together. This creates stress all around the object. But propping can help. You have to have another mold made and with it pour another shape in which to rest the vase. This is called a setter.

Since most mold company molds are made for ceramics, you have to be quite choosey about the items you are going to use, because setters for mold-poured greenware are unavailable, except for plates or dinnerware.

A vase, however, can be turned upside down and rested on the top rim, as the top usually has a stronger shape. If it is balanced and the kiln is level it will fire properly. But only testing and cautious firing will have it turn out all right.

If you feel your cast piece would be oddly shaped, and the weight is not evenly divided, you had better not use it—unless you want to do some adventurous firing. That's the only way you will know for sure.

SIZE OF MOLD

If you are strong and have no body ailments, mold size probably will not matter to you. But some molds can be quite heavy for someone who, because of a heart condition or arthritis, has back problems or should not lift anything heavy.

So, be careful about the mold size that you choose.

PRESS MOLDS

Press molds, which I use, are for making different flowers. The forms are made of fired ceramic bisque (see pages 156, 157 for press mold). Clay is pulled over the form and then refined so it has a smooth elegant look.

These press molds can be fired at the ceramic firing, cone 06, after they have been washed in water. This will make them like new again if they become dirty. They are inexpensive and are very helpful for extensive creating.

CUTTERS

I also use metal cutters to make flowers. There are some with handles to push out the clay, and others that are like cookie cutters. Both are very good for flower-making techniques. These are used only with clay (see page 60 for clay making).

LEAF IMPRESSION FORMS

These forms are green in color and are made of rubber. They are formed in all leaf shapes and they have every vein line for realistic impressions. These are also used with clay. They are superb in quality, and with your added touch you can make beautiful leaves for flowers and other ornate creations (see pages 68, 72 for leaf forms).

PREPARING
THE MOLD FOR POURING

DRYING THE MOLD

When molds are newly wet or saturated from pouring, always dry them banded together. Make sure they are tightly locked together, or they may dry out of shape and become warped.

Mold companies will advise against this, but when I have a very damp mold I set it on high posts on top of the closed kiln while firing. This will allow the heat to circulate around the mold and inside when turned upside down. When drying like this, make sure the mold is not set directly on the heat. As long as the heat is allowed to surround the whole mold it will dry evenly. Remember to do this only when you are firing. Otherwise you will be wasting electricity just for drying.

If you don't need a mold right away, set it out in the warm sun. It should dry in a few days, depending on the size of the mold. This is really the best way, but it does take a bit longer.

A fan blowing directly on a mold also is effective. It will allow the air to circulate, and this may be the only way to dry the mold if the sun is not shining or it is winter and cold outside.

As I stated in the preceding section, some mold companies do dry molds for you on request, and thus when you collect the mold it is ready to pour.

REMEDYING A WARPED MOLD

If a mold becomes warped, saturate it in water. Then set it on a flat table or floor with a heavy weight resting on top of it. The heavier the weight the better. The stress of the weight will flatten the warpage and lock the joints together. When you notice that it is in proper condition, again, make sure that it is banded with extra bands to make it tight enough so it will not go out of shape again.

CLEANING THE MOLD

When the mold is dry enough to pour, take it apart and make sure all the dust and dirt particles are cleaned away. Using a soft brush, push the dirt up and out of the mold. Any residue left inside will cause imperfections in the cast piece—it will stick to the ware. When the piece is fired, the dirt will disintegrate, leaving small pit marks and holes where the dirt had been. This will leave a bad surface for painting or decorating.

Once all dirt is removed, take a sponge and clean out any dirt marks on the plaster. If it is not a new mold and has been used for earthenware, sponge off the whole mold, inside and out. Since earthenware is fired at a lower temperature, the mold must be cleaned before it is used with porcelain clay, which is fired at a higher temperature. The two clays do not mix.

Sponge the mold with denatured alcohol. This evaporates as soon as it cleans, so it will not saturate the mold.

BANDING THE MOLD

After you have cleaned the mold reband it again. Make sure you have enough rubber bands on it to make it very tight. If not, the pressure of the liquid slip inside will push on the mold, causing the slip to gush out through the seams.

If you let this happen the casting will have extreme seam lines. You don't want them. The fewer seam lines the better it will be to clean the greenware and make the seams unnoticeable.

The best thing to remember when banding a mold is always to put more bands on the mold than you think you will need. Then you will not have to worry about any accidents.

Before using a mold for casting, make sure that all the dirt and dust are removed from the inside of the mold. Be careful not to injure the mold impression. Using a soft brush or ceramic duster mop is best.

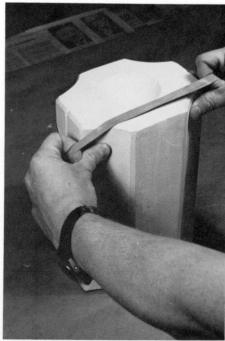

SEPARATING A MOLD WHEN IT STICKS

Some new molds, wet and dry, may stick together and become inseparable. If you try to pry the mold apart you may break or chip the keys that lock the mold together.

Run some water over the mold where the parts join, and then slap the sides. This will usually separate the mold. If not, take a plastic cleaning tool and lay it across the joint. Tap on the tool, sending it carefully into the joint, and the mold should separate. Be careful to hold the mold parts so when they come apart they do not fall and break.

PORCELAIN SLIP
AND ITS DESIRED PURPOSE

WHAT IS PORCELAIN

Porcelain was first produced by the Chinese thousands of years ago from mixtures of special clays and minerals. These properties led to high-fire porcelains, lending themselves to delicate shapes and figures. Their formula was a safely guarded secret. As years went by, other countries mastered their own mixtures and concoctions. Feldspar, quartz, kaolin, and even bone ash are mixed to make porcelain slips. But everyone has his own recipe.

Because there are many types of porcelain mixes, it is up to you to select the right type for you. There are many porcelain manufacturers who produce it by the gallon for the ceramic hobbyists. They are all good for certain purposes, but some work better than others.

To decide which is best suited for you, you have to decide what you want to do with it. Before that, you have to know what the porcelain can do for you.

There are many factors that the craftsman must consider in a porcelain slip. One is translucency. Porcelain is translucent when the bisque-fired porcelain allows light to pass through. It lends itself well, for instance, to lamps with lightable bases. Translucent dinnerware is also created with a fine translucent slip. Without this, dinnerware would be opaque and less sparkly.

Not all porcelains are translucent. You have to make sure by either asking the manufacturer for a sample piece or by test-firing a cast piece yourself. Testing in your own kiln and firing may be better for you in the long run, since different firing conditions can alter the condition of the fired piece.

For pieces that you intend to fully decorate and paint make sure the porcelain is a beautiful white when fired. If it is an off-white you may

---

← After the mold is cleaned, band it with heavy-duty rubber bands. They can be purchased at almost any ceramic shop. Make sure enough bands are around the mold to secure the seam tightly or slip will flow through the joinings, making unsightly seam lines.

have to paint white china paint on the porcelain to get it white. But the white portions on the creation should be the porcelain white, not china painted white. The true look of porcelain occurs when you can see a part of the porcelain unpainted—and that includes any unpainted area of the structural piece.

Use the whitest porcelain you can find. The off-white color may be suitable for some things, but for items needing pure-white areas, don't settle for less than snow-white porcelain.

Your slip should set up moderately, not too fast. If it sets up too fast the casting will get too thick. Sometimes it takes too long to set up, wasting precious time. If this happens, then you know the mixture was incorrect. Porcelain has a quicker set-up time than earthenware clays. Porcelain should set up in about three to five minutes for translucent thin castings, and five to six minutes for thicker, heavier castings.

You also want to make sure of the shrinking factor. Porcelain shrinks some when high-fired; some porcelains shrink quite a bit more than others when fired, and you don't want too much loss in size. Again, the only way you will know is by asking the manufacturer for a sample piece tested for shrinkage. Better yet, test-fire again on your own. However, companies should be able to tell you what percentage of shrinkage to expect.

When firing porcelain, sagging and cracking may occur. This is another problem to watch for, and I have to stress again that the only way you will know for sure is to test-fire something yourself. There are some mixtures that will not stand up to high-firing. If continuous cracking and sagging occur, change porcelains.

Don't get me wrong—there will be some sagging and small cracks, but when they become so extreme that you can see them clearly, something needs adjusting. Small objects should not sag or crack at all unless there is a slight curvature in the shape of the object. But a good porcelain, when fired correctly, will not sag or crack perceptibely.

When some porcelain is fired, black spots occur on the porcelain bisque. These are caused by impurities in the clays and minerals. If these spots keep occurring, and if the company supplying the porcelain does not investigate the problem, change to another porcelain. There is nothing more irritating than making a piece and firing it to bisque and then discovering black spots.

There are colored porcelains that come in pastel blue, pink, yellow, green, deep Wedgwood blue, green, black, brown, and many other colors and shades. Flesh colors are very convenient for those who want an overall flesh color for a figurine. Colors are also useful when you want to double cast a piece to produce two colors on one object (see double casting, page 32).

So remember, when selecting your porcelain, to keep all these factors in mind; otherwise you may create a beautiful piece and end up with a badly fired defective mess.

POURING (CASTING)

PREPARING YOUR PORCELAIN

After you have prepared the mold for pouring (sponging, cleaning, and banding securely), then you must prepare your porcelain.

When you open up your container of porcelain you will find that it may be thick and lumpy, with a watery residue on top. This has to be mixed thoroughly and blended to a creamy consistency. Any thickness or lumps will cause poor castings. The best way to really blend it well is to use a rotor mixer or even a cake mixer. There are many other types of mixers available at ceramic supply distributors.

For the beginner it would be best to start using porcelain from the gallon jug. This will require only a small mixer. Mix and beat the porcelain well till it is of a light creamy consistency. If it is still thick, add a small amount of water and remix.

After it is mixed, strain the slip so any lumps may be found and discarded.

After the slip is mixed ánd strained, let it stand a few minutes so the air trapped in it during the mixing escapes from the slip. Otherwise, when casting, you will have pit marks from the air holes. If you tap the container a few times that will usually release the air sooner.

For large multiple castings there are pouring bins. They hold a larger quantity of slip; some have a capacity of more than fifty gallons. The pouring table is built above the bin so the slip will run back down into the bin. Dowels are spaced at intervals across the top of the pouring bin and allow the slip to pass through when the molds rest upside down on the dowels. The pouring setup also has a pouring spout like a gas hose. This allows faster pouring from mold to mold. All you have to do is set the molds on the dowel tabletop, pour them, and turn them over and let them drain. Thus there is little handling of the molds, especially when they are too large to lift easily.

These bins can be bought at manufacturers' outlets or at ceramic shop distributors. The prices range from two hundred dollars up, depending on the size and capacity of the tank.

If pouring with a gallon jug, which most of you will be doing, you will have to carefully drain the excess slip back into the jug in order not to waste it.

When you are sure the porcelain slip is smooth, with no lumps, and of a creamy consistency, you are ready to pour your castings.

BASIC POURING

When pouring into the mold always pour directly into the center of the pour-gate hole so slip falls into the bottom of the mold first, filling from bottom to top. Any slip that dribbles into the mold while pouring may leave pour marks in the ware. Make sure you are pouring continuously till the mold is filled to the top of the pour-gate hole. If you stop it will cause a separation line where you stopped and began again.

As the slip moisture is absorbed in the mold plaster, the slip pour-gate line will recede. Make sure you keep it filled to the top so you can determine how thick the casting is.

The casting thickness is decided by cutting away an edge of the clay in the pour-gate hole. The thickness you see is the thickness of the whole casting inside the mold. Make sure that you pour it out a little before it reaches the thickness required, because the excess slip remaining inside the casting will also add a bit of thickness.

Pouring out the slip will create a hollow casting; otherwise the slip remaining inside the mold would cause the object to become solid. Solid pieces are not acceptable. When fired they could explode, destroying all the objects in the kiln.

When you are pouring out the slip, make sure you pour it out with an even flow. Don't just turn it over and let it gush out. A sudden gush could cause a vacuum inside the mold and the casting walls would collapse. When draining the mold, turn it around so there is no excess slip lying in a deep crevice. Any excess will cause the ware to stay wet longer.

After all the excess is out turn the mold over and prop it upside down on kiln shelf posts. This will allow the air to circulate inside the mold, hardening and drying the casting. The casting should set up in about ten to twenty minutes. Let it dry in the mold until it is fully dried and firm enough to hold its own weight. If this is not done, when the casting is set up and out of the mold it will probably collapse.

Once it has drooped and fallen out of shape there is nothing you can do to make it right again. For there is one very interesting and important truth about porcelain: *It has a memory.* Whatever happens to it during casting becomes permanent. So, if you pull an object out of shape, you cannot by any method persuade it to resume the shape it held before firing.

There is another factor to remember: When the casting is in the mold it is actually shrinking a bit as the water is absorbed from the slip. Thus, if you leave it in the mold too long the undercuts and grooves will grab the ware, causing cracks to occur when removing the piece. So use your judgment and leave the work in the mold only long enough for it to set up strong enough to manage its weight. If not, you will have cracking problems.

After the casting is set up to your desire, you must clean the pour-gate hole of the mold and remove the excess slip on the top of the mold. Use a fettling knife and cut easily around the hole and deep enough into the funnel shape. Cut the area so the hole is perfectly smooth. If it has jagged edges, it will cause cracking when drying.

After the pour-gate hole is cleaned, you may take the rubber bands off. Remove them carefully, making sure the mold is still held together by your hands or the mold may fall apart. Set it up straight and then slap the sides lightly. If the cast is ready to come out, the mold parts will release and come apart.

Set the mold on its side so the mold parts can be lifted from one another. This will prevent mold parts from falling and breaking.

If the mold has more than two parts, remember which parts to release in what order. The mold usually has marks on it advising when and in which direction to release each mold part. If not, you must know this before you cast the piece, so number the mold parts with a marker to help you know in which order to release the parts after casting.

Lift the top part off carefully in case something may still stick. If it comes up easily keep lifting straight up. It should be all right. After the mold is apart, let the casting rest in the mold part for a few minutes until it is hard enough to stand on its own. Just make sure you don't leave it in the mold too long. Remember that if it shrinks too much it may grab at grooves and crevices, causing cracks.

Casting Materials: from left to right, water and sponge, jug of porcelain slip, fettling knife, double-ended cleaning tool, brush, plastic mold-cleaning tool, slip mixer, and paper toweling for cleaning.

Mix the slip with the mixer and then strain the slip through a strainer to get rid of any large lumps that may have accumulated.

After it has dried long enough, take a wet sponge and smooth any holes that may be on the bottom of the ware. Hold the ware lightly so as not to push it out of shape. Set it on a paper or cardboard to dry. The paper will keep the ware from sticking to the table where it is resting. Some objects do require cleaning while still leather-hard (moist), so they should be stored in a damp box (any container with a lid). This is covered in a later chapter.

Pour the slip into the mold slowly and continue a steady flow to fill to the top of the pour-gate hole. Never stop, or lines will appear where starting and stopping occurred.

Make sure the pour-gate hole is filled to the top to ensure the proper thickness of the casting.

When slip recedes, fill up again.

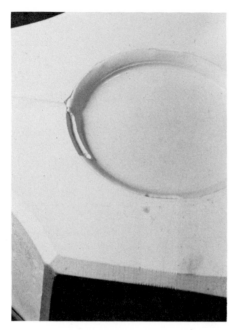

To see how thick the casting is in the mold, cut, with cleaning tool, a section of the top of the pour-gate hole. This will allow you to see how thick the casting is becoming.

After casting time is over, pour the excess slip back into the jug. Do this slowly and steadily or a vacuum may occur, causing the inside cast walls to collapse, thus ruining the cast.

After the removal of the slip, prop the mold pour-gate hole down on posts from the kiln to allow air to circulate up and through the mold.

Using the plastic cleaning tool, clean away any excess hard clay from the top of the mold. The plastic tool will protect the mold from being gouged or damaged while cleaning.

Using a fettling knife, carefully cut the clay from the pour gate before you open the mold.

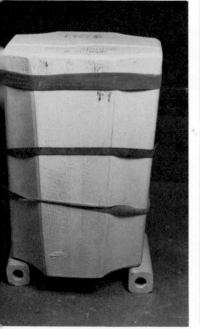

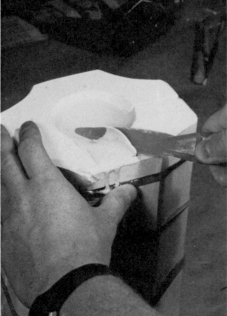

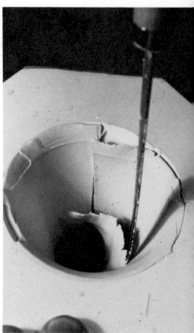

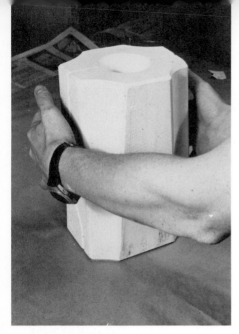

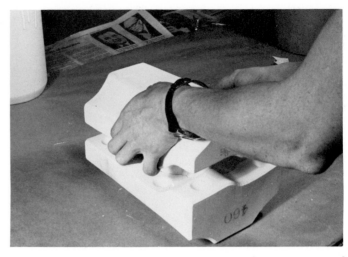

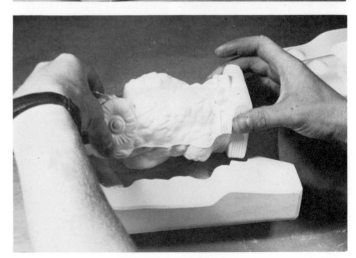

After the rubber bands are taken off the mold, set the mold up and slap the sides. This will allow the casting inside to release itself for removal.

Set the mold flat to remove the mold top. Lift gently in case the casting sticks. If it does, let it sit a few more minutes to allow more drying, then try again.

Let the casting sit in the mold till it is positively dry enough to remove without causing it to go out of shape.

Remove the casting with both hands to avoid dropping the piece.

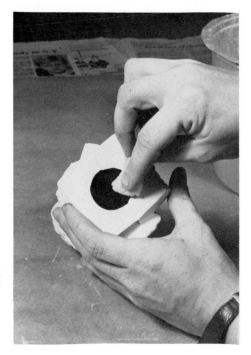

After removal of the piece, sponge the hole on the bottom so it is perfectly smooth. Any rough edges will crack while drying and firing.

The casting after all seam lines have been cleaned.

TRANSLUCENT CASTING

A translucent casting is a piece of ware that has been cast thin enough to allow light to pass through it. The porcelain also has a lot to do with it, but the thinner the casting the more translucent it becomes when fired.

This type of casting is used for lamps and night-lights. Light passing through creates a sparkly look that enhances any lamplight. There are also lamps whose bases are lit up with a light, thus needing the translucency.

China dinnerware also is finished in translucent thinness. Some dinnerwares are so translucent that you can pass your hand behind a piece and see a very sharp shadow. This translucency increases the value of quite a number of porcelain objects.

(31)

DOUBLE CASTING

Many people who have worked with porcelain probably have never heard of double casting. It is done usually with a light- and a dark-colored porcelain cast one on top of the other.

If you have a basket mold and want it white inside and pink on the outside you would double cast it; otherwise you would have to paint it those colors.

In double casting, you first pour in the colored slip which, when cast, will be the outside color of the basket. Leave this pouring in about two to three minutes, then pour the excess slip out, making sure you pour that slip into the container holding the right color.

Let this cast set until the slip is altogether dry. Now take the white slip and pour the mold full again. Leave it in about the same time again, then pour it back out. After this, follow the procedures for taking out your casting.

This type of casting lends itself well for objects with inside and outside areas that are seen together, such as vases, dishes, ashtrays, and the like.

STICK-ONS

After you have all the castings made for your piece, there may be parts that need to be attached to the main structure. These parts are called stick-ons. If there are quite a few of them it is best to store them in a damp box to keep them moist, because stick-ons need to be moist to adhere properly. The box can be made of plastic or hard rubber, and should have a lid to close it airtight. Plastic shoe boxes come in various sizes and serve this purpose well.

Put the pieces into the box and close tightly. If you cannot put the pieces together immediately after casting, the box will keep them moist till ready. However, if you leave them in the box for more than a few days they may dry out. Adding a wet sponge or cloth will sometimes keep them moist longer.

Before doing any attaching, you must clean all seam lines. The reason to clean while the pieces are still moist (leather-hard) is that when there are stick-ons the piece is more fragile. If you try to clean the piece when it is dry and stuck together, it will be brittle and will break.

After all the seam lines are cleaned and sponged, take your cutting tool and cut a hole into any area that is to receive a stick-on. This allows ventilation when firing and permits the escape of gases that would cause the piece to explode. If there are no holes in the base, put a small hole in it somewhere to allow for gas escapage. Make sure the holes are sponged so they are not rough.

After all the cuts are made you are ready to attach. Brush slip on all the areas to be joined. Make sure enough slip is on them so it will seep through the joints. Push the pieces together and hold them tight as the slip runs out. You will have to hold it a few seconds to make sure it is stuck securely; then you can let it go.

After the part has adhered well, take a brush and apply some slip around where it is joined so the attachment line is covered. If it does not cover it well, take some porcelain clay and smear it over the joint to camouflage the area. Take your cleaning tool and push it into the crevice. Let it dry a few minutes, then smooth it with a wet sponge. This can make a bad joining line disappear.

If the piece is elaborate you will want to create it on a kiln shelf from the beginning. This will prevent your breaking the piece while transferring it to the shelf after completion. Propping will also be necessary if the overhanging parts are extensive (see pages 40, 41 for propping).

Many molds must be poured when stick-ons are needed for a creation. Here four are needed to assemble a small kitten.

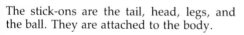
The stick-ons are the tail, head, legs, and the ball. They are attached to the body.

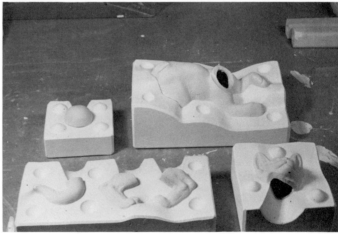

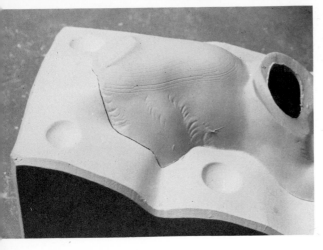

Depending on how the slip is poured, air sometimes will get trapped inside the mold, causing air lines to occur on the casting.

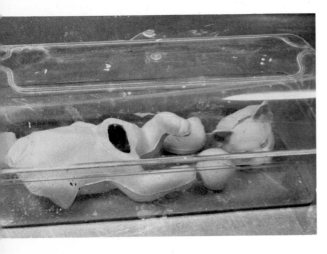

When creating pieces with stick-ons, enclose the pieces in a damp box to keep them moist for attaching. A plastic shoe box is usually the ideal size.

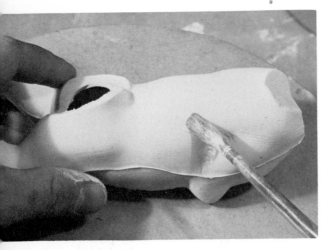

The lines from the air pockets can be covered over with slip. Apply with a soft brush until lines are fully covered.

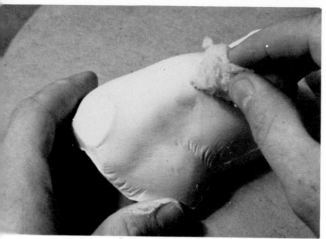

Take a moist sponge and smooth over the added slip so there is no trace of the lines.

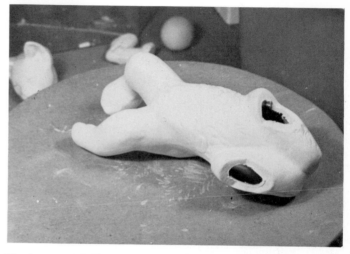

The two areas where the legs are to be attached must have holes cut in them to allow any gases to escape from the legs.

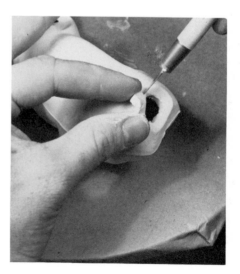

The flat area for the tail must also be cut, for tail attachment.

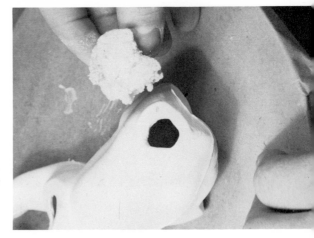

Sponge all the areas that were cut for assemblage so no rough edges are left for cracking.

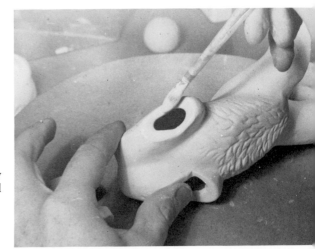

After all seam lines are cleaned on the body and legs, apply some slip onto the leg and body area where attachment is to be made.

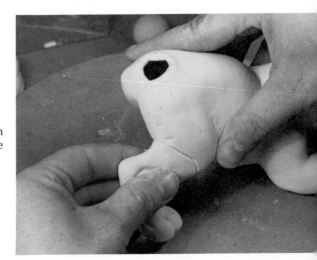

Press leg stick-on onto the body location and hold a few seconds till you are sure the adhesion is secure.

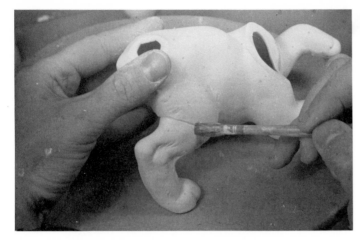

Apply more slip over the area where joined, to make sure of a perfect attachment.

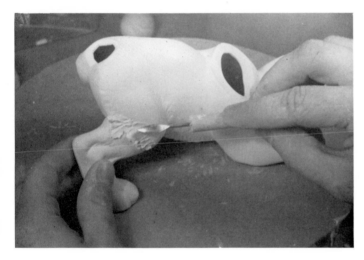

To cover up the joining groove, apply some clay with the cleaning tool and press into the joining.

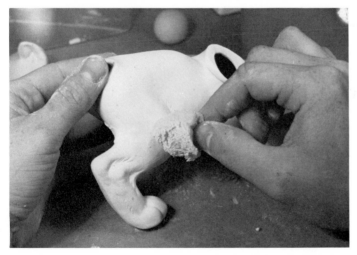

Take a moist sponge and wipe lightly over the clay to smooth out the roughness and blend into the rest of the cat's body.

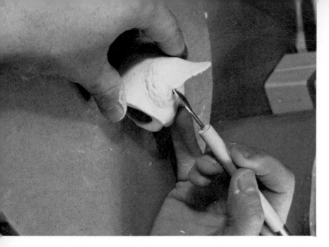

Clean the seam lines on the cat's head and tail for attaching.

Sponge over all seam lines so they are smooth and clean.

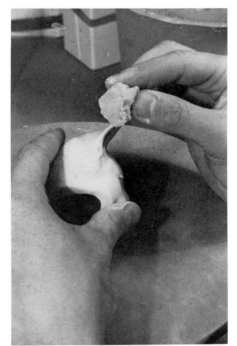

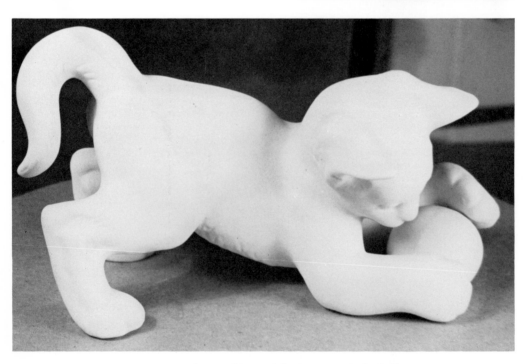

Final assemblage of the kitten with the ball.

CLEANING GREENWARE

WET GREENWARE

Elaborate creations must be cleaned when the parts are being put together. Once a piece is dried completely the porcelain is so brittle that just a sudden jarring of the table could demolish it. Cleaning the piece while it is wet will be safer.

When cleaning wet greenware, take your cleaning tool with the curved or straight end and drag it along the seam line. Make sure you do not dig into the clay because this might cause the seam line to pop up during the firing; all you want to do is clean away the seam line so there is no excessive clay visible. Then take a wet sponge and drag it lightly across the cleaned area. Make sure the sponge is only slightly moist, because too much water will cause the sponge to leave marks.

Make sure that any small holes or pit marks (air-bubble holes) are covered. While the piece is still wet take some moist clay and press it into the hole, forcing out the air. Then sponge over it. Any marks or slip runs should be sponged also.

When cleaning dried greenware, hold the piece gently. With a piece as solid as this you should have no trouble, but with ornate pieces very careful cleaning must be done.

After cleaning all seam lines, sponge all cleaned areas smooth. Also sponge over any flaws or marks that may have accidentally happened during pouring.

DRIED GREENWARE

Cleaning dried greenware is basically the same as cleaning wet greenware except for the sponging. After you have cleaned the seam lines, use a paper towel or a nylon stocking to rub over the cleaned areas to smooth them out. Take a sponge and wipe over the areas to remove any powdery residue left from cleaning. If necessary you can use a sponge lightly to smooth even more.

Pit holes and marks also need filling. To do this, drip water from your finger into the hole. Then take some completely dried greenware clay scraps, crush them into powder, and fill the hole with it. The water you dripped into the hole will make this moist and allow it to fill up and force out the air. Make sure you fill the hole completely. Otherwise the piece may still have a slight indentation when it is fired.

As I said before, dried greenware is very brittle and fragile. Hold it gently, letting it rest in your hands, because even a slight pressure will cause the piece to crumble. After cleaning, put the work on a kiln shelf. This will keep it from having to be handled and from being broken.

CONE 018 FIRED GREENWARE

For people who are afraid to clean wet or dried greenware another step may be taken, although it cannot be made with elaborate creations because of their fragility.

The porcelain piece can be fired at cone 018 to make the ware harder and less breakable. It fires it just enough to harden it so that it can be held more firmly.

The piece is cleaned the same way as before, but a grit rubber scrubber of the finest grade is used to sand down seam lines and to make them smooth. The scrubber has sponge on one side and fine sand paper on the other.

PROPPING FOR FIRING

You may ask what propping is and why it is needed. When porcelain is fired in the kiln, the temperature reaches such a high level that the porcelain actually does things you wouldn't imagine.

It becomes soft, it shrinks, and it moves, making propping necessary. Without it, any extending parts such as arms, legs, branches, or birds with open wings, would become soft and sag. To prevent this, support is needed.

PROPS MADE OF PORCELAIN

Props used to hold up the extending parts also have to be made of porcelain so that when the piece shrinks the prop shrinks accordingly. If not, the piece is pushed out of shape because the prop would stay exactly where it was while the shrinkage occurred.

The props may be made in any shape, but they must not be thick. Remember, solid things fired will possibly explode. The props should be hollowed slightly to prevent this. When using porcelain props, flint wash should be brushed on the props to keep them from adhering to the creation. If this wash is not used the props cannot be removed. (See page 63 for Flint Wash.)

PROPPING WITH CERAMIC FIBER

For those of you who want an easier way to prop, there is a ceramic fiber suitable for all firing. Once you use it you will need nothing else. It is a cottonlike substance that can be pushed into any shape and can withstand the heat of the kiln. It also adapts readily, shrinking as the piece shrinks. It isn't really costly because it can be reused quite a few times before it must be discarded. Porcelain props must be thrown away after a single use. When propping an elaborate piece, make sure you do not stuff the propping material too tightly under areas or there will not be any room for the fiber to push together, causing the piece to fire out of shape.

Not everything needs propping, but any extending parts do. When firing boxes or pieces with lids you will also have to stuff the box with fiber so the lid does not sag in (firing boxes, see page 63).

Prop an elaborate piece while it is still wet, leather-hard. If it is propped when bone dry the fiber cannot be stuffed under the areas without breaking the piece.

Remember, any extensive propping should be done while the piece is still slightly wet.

This is ceramic fiber. It is actually a heating substance from stoves, but since it can withstand heat it has become the means for propping and supporting porcelain during high-firing.

A face mask like this is recommended when working with ceramic fiber because the fiber can cause you to cough if it is inhaled. However, it is not dangerous.

THE KILN

Many of you may have never seen or fired a kiln, but for those of you who have, bear with me.

A ceramic kiln is an oven that can reach temperatures as high as 2300 degrees Fahrenheit. It can be used for many different projects such as ceramic earthenware, glass sagging, enameling, and porcelain and china painting.

Today most kilns are factory made and can be purchased in different sizes, although they all still fire up to the same temperatures. Some people cannot use large kilns so the smaller hobby kilns are ideal for them. There are even kilns so small that they can fire only one piece at a time. These are definitely for the apartment dweller.

Most of the kilns can be separated into three or four sections depending on size. The sections rest on top of one another, making moving more convenient. Each section is light in weight, but, combined, they make a kiln quite heavy, even though they are made of lightweight firebrick.

The kilns take a 220-volt line, which is usually the same as that used by an electric range or clothes washer. Some kilns are now being made to plug into a regular wall socket. They are supposed to fire up to porcelain firing. You must read your owner's manual so you may fully understand the electrical parts and the installation of the kiln, because every kiln is different and has its own setup.

Kilns can be bought with kiln "sitters" on them. These are convenient automatic shutoffs. The sitter will shut the kiln off when it reaches the desired temperature. Some kilns also have timers that you can set for the length of time you think the kiln will need to fire. If the sitter by any chance does not shut it off, the timer will.

There are manual shut-off kilns, but, for a little more money, you can have the automatic convenience.

The object that indicates the time for the shutoff is called the cone. This is a small cone-shaped object made of a substance that will melt and bend at a desired temperature. There are different ones for all the needed firing temperatures.

The kiln sitter has a rod leading into the kiln from the box hooked outside the kiln. The cone rests on the rod inside the cylinder. When it reaches the indicated temperature the small rod falls down and the lever outside the kiln falls down, shutting off the kiln. It is almost foolproof, unless a malfunction occurs.

A kiln should never be left alone for long, especially when you know about the time it should shut off. If it doesn't, you can shut it off manually.

If this should occur, you will not really know if the desired temperature has been reached unless you have a pyrometer, an instrument with a wire that leads into the kiln and tells you the exact temperature inside the kiln. With this you know if the right level of heat has been reached.

There are many different brands of kilns so I cannot name all of them. But most are reputable.

The types I recommend have a gradation in the switch controls. Some have only low, medium, and high, but I prefer those that also have numbered gradations, for the times you may want to have more control over your firing schedule.

Most kilns when firing do not stay on continuously. They heat on and off to build up the heat gradually. So the electric kiln isn't really so bad as most people think (see firing, page 48). There are gas kilns available, but I have never used one. Because electric kilns are so convenient it is more sensible to use them.

The electric kilns use coils to relay heat in the oven. If a coil should malfunction, it can be replaced. If a firebrick cracks or chips it, too, can be replaced. A kiln should last years if maintained and used correctly.

Most kilns cost anywhere from $150 to $700 or $800. There will always be the best one for your needs, large or small.

Electric kilns are used to fire porcelain. Depending on the sizes of the kilns, they can be taken apart in different sections.

Inside the kiln are coils that heat up red hot during firing. Each section of coils has its own control.

The firebrick, of which the walls are made, holds the heat inside the kiln. The outside is covered with sheet metal, which holds the brick together.

This is the kiln sitter actuating rod, which automatically shuts off the kiln when the desired temperature is reached.

The cone is inserted in the resting part of the rod, which leads to the outside part of the sitter, which falls to shut off the kiln.

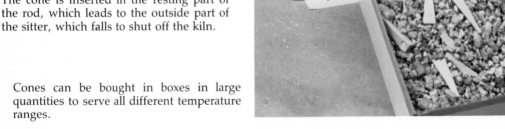

Cones can be bought in boxes in large quantities to serve all different temperature ranges.

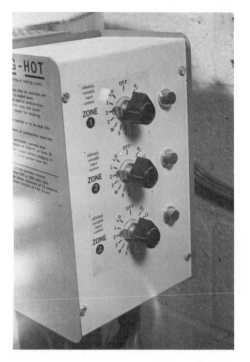

The part of the kiln sitter located outside the kiln has the timer dial on it. When the little black claw rises the metal flap falls, shutting off the kiln. Proper use of the sitter should be learned from careful reading of the manufacturer's manual.

Controls on a kiln are usually set up to control each section of coils throughout the kiln. Controls usually have the low, medium, and high switches; some have the different gradation numbers to be used for slower firing.

KILN FURNITURE

The materials needed for stacking your kiln are called furniture.
Shelves. The shelves are made of the same firebrick as that in the kiln, except that it has been pressed harder. It can withstand the heat. The shelves are used to stack objects of porcelain in the kiln in many ways and come in different sizes and shapes to fit your kiln—round, square, half shelves, whole shelves, even octagonal.

Shelves for the kiln come in many different shapes and sizes. There are also half shelves, which allow for stacking of higher pieces in certain areas of the kiln.

Posts. Posts are used to divide the kiln into different shelf layers. The kiln shelves rest on these posts. They also come in many lengths, so that sections of space between stacked shelves can be different.

Stilts. Many ceramists know of stilts as kiln furniture. But in porcelain work they are not used at all. In ceramics their pieces rest on these so as not to touch the shelf and stick when glazed. If porcelain pieces were set on these stilts, the pointed prongs would poke through the porcelain during the firing.

Posts for the shelf dividing can be bought in many different heights and shapes. They allow a variety of divisions between firing shelves.

Shelves can be stacked in many different ways, using the posts and shelves.

Half shelves are also used so that one side of a shelf has more height for higher pieces.

PREPARING FOR FIRING

The first thing to do is to make the kiln level—*perfectly* level. Any uneven slant will make the porcelain object sag or lean.

The kiln must be cleaned of all dirt and dust. Take a sweeper with a brush end and suck all the dirt out. Any dust or dirt in the kiln will float around and will eventually bake into the porcelain, causing imperfections.

Shelves and posts should also be cleaned. Even the undersides of the shelves must be cleaned because any dirt there will fall onto the objects below.

STACKING SHELVES

Shelves are used to stack porcelain pieces in layers in the kiln. Before setting the pieces on the kiln shelves, kiln-wash the shelves. The wash material can be bought at any ceramic or kiln dealer. It is a powdered substance to be mixed with water and then brushed over the top of each shelf. You must make sure, also, that the floor of the kiln is washed.

Next, sprinkle flint powder on the shelves before resting the porcelain pieces there. This powder keeps the porcelain from sticking to the shelves and prevents heat shock from the shelves from splitting the porcelain bottoms.

When filling the kiln do not set pieces on the kiln floor because the heat at the floor level never becomes intense enough to permit the pieces to mature to porcelain on the bottoms where they rest, but leaves them a chalky white.

Put posts at least two inches high on the floor and place a shelf on top of them. This will allow the heat to circulate under the shelf, heating the bottoms of the porcelain properly.

Always make sure you have at least two heating coils between the shelf separations, to allow the heat to circulate evenly throughout the kiln. Many shelves can be stacked as long as enough heat reaches the pieces. If not, the porcelain will not mature.

Half shelves can be used, leaving more space on one side to accommodate a taller piece. Any combinations are acceptable.

Unlike earthenware, porcelain pieces dare not touch one another during firing or they will fuse together permanently.

Items that need to be fired together, but not permanently, must have flint wash applied to those areas that touch to keep them from sticking. After the firing this material can be brushed off and the areas wiped with water (see page 63 for flint wash).

When stacking, it is best to put the larger pieces on the bottom

(47)

When filling the kiln, make sure that no pieces touch during firing. Unlike ceramic earthenware, porcelain pieces will fuse together wherever touching. So make sure there is enough space between each piece and its neighbor.

When first beginning to fire, prop the lid open two to three inches till gases are fully released from kiln. Also leave out the top peephole plug during the first few hours of firing.

shelves and the smaller pieces on the top shelves, keeping items of the same size together. In this way all the pieces will receive the same amount of heat.

FIRING

Basic firing: Firing is a crucial and important part of porcelain-making. Firing can make the difference between a perfect piece and a damaged piece.

The first thing to consider is the object you are firing. There are two firings involved in finishing a porcelain piece. The high firing reaches 2300 degrees, or cone 6. This temperature changes the greenware porcelain to bisque. The second firing, the low or gold firing, reaches 1300 to 1400 degrees, or cone 018-019, for china-paint firing, otherwise known as overglaze firing.

There is one other firing, called the glaze firing. It reaches 1859 degrees, or cone 06. Sometimes, if high-fire glaze is used, the cone 2 is used, reaching a higher temperature for maturity.

When using a kiln sitter (see pages 42, 43, 44, 45 for sitter), always use the next higher cone than that required in a manually operated kiln, because of mechanical leeway in setup. The actuating rod creates weight on the cone, causing it to fall sooner, and the higher cone allows for this difference.

Put a two- or three-inch post under the handle of the lid of the kiln to prop the lid slightly open. Leave the top peephole plug open. This will permit the air to circulate through the hole and out the top of the kiln, releasing all gases and fumes.

It is best to let greenware porcelain dry at least twenty-four hours before firing it to mature bisque. If it is wet when it is fired, the heat can cause it to explode because the fumes and gases cannot escape fast enough.

If you have to fire it while it is wet, to get faster production, you will have to low-fire it for a longer period. This will allow the ware to dry gradually.

SIMPLIFIED FIRING SCHEDULES

Porcelain high-firing: Use a cone 6 in manual operation, cone 7 if kiln sitter is used. Make sure cone is properly set up. Follow owner's kiln manual. Prop lid open about two to three inches with top peephole out.

1. Put all switches on low for three hours.

2. Turn all switches to medium for four hours. During this time if the fumes have stopped coming out of kiln (smell above the kiln opening), close the lid slowly and put the peephole plug in.

3. Turn all switches to high. The kiln should shut off in about four to five hours after the last turn. The total approximate time is ten to twelve hours, depending on the type of kiln used.

4. It is also best to keep watch to see how long the firing is actually taking. If the heat gets excessive it is best to shut off the kiln. If a kiln overfires the pieces can melt to a blob on the shelves and destroy all the shelves and possibly ruin your kiln.

Watch the pyrometer so you do not overfire. This instrument will tell you the inside temperature of the kiln. If the kiln does not shut off automatically, the pyrometer will tell you when the desired temperature has been reached, so you can shut off the kiln manually.

Porcelain-firing simple objects: When firing one-piece objects, there are no deep crevices or deep areas where moisture will hide, so most of the wetness is evaporated easily. This allows a little faster firing since there is no long firing needed for areas to dry.

1. Turn all switches to low for about two hours. Prop lid open with top peephole plug out.

2. Turn all switches to medium for about three hours. Close lid when all fumes and smell are gone. Close the peephole plug.

3. Turn all switches to high. The kiln should shut off in from four to five hours. Total hours' firing, approximately ten hours or less.

China-paint firing: China-paint firing is basically the same except for the temperature change and firing time.

1. Turn all switches to low for one hour. Prop lid open with top peephole open.

2. After one hour in low turn all switches to medium. Close lid AFTER FUMES HAVE SUBSIDED. PUT IN PEEPHOLE PLUG.

3. After one hour on medium turn all to high. Kiln will shut off in about three or four hours.

Glaze firing: The procedure used here is the same as with porcelain firing except for the switch controls. The cone used is cone 06 or 05. If high-fire glaze is used, fire to cone 2 (see glazing and firing, page 115).

After kiln has shut off: After pieces are fired and kiln shuts off let the kiln cool for from ten to twelve hours before lifting lid. Then prop the lid open about six inches to let the heat rise slowly out of the kiln and cool it down gradually. Otherwise the cool air will cause the pieces to split and ping. An hour or so later open the lid wide, but do not remove the pieces until you can pick them out with your bare fingers.

When you take them out clean or brush the flint from the bottoms of the pieces. And the ceramic fiber will have to be pulled and brushed clean, using a ceramic duster mop.

I recommend the use of a face mask (paint mask) while brushing the ceramic fiber so you don't breathe in any (see page 41). It could make you cough, and the mask can prevent that.

When brushing off the ceramic fiber, take care not to accidentally break anything off the elaborate pieces.

Refining the pieces: After cleaning the pieces, brush them with a 100 grit rubber scrubber or a fine grade of sandpaper to remove any excess porcelain dust, making the pieces very smooth and in the ideal condition for painting with china paints. The pieces will keep their soft and clean look.

Some pieces may have a few slight cracks or crevices. These can be filled with sculpture paste, which can be thinned with water. Fill the crack and let some excess paste remain outside the crack. Then use your cleaning tool to scrape away the excess, and sand with a fine grade of sandpaper. This will hide the crack. This must be done after the china-paint firing. To cover the area fixed, touch up with flat or glossy enamel paints. These can be bought at most hobby shops. The colors are varied and are referred to as glossies or flats. They also work perfectly for all touch-ups where colors may not have fired correctly, and they will cover sculpture paste too.

2

PORCELAIN TECHNIQUES

SGRAFFITO

Sgraffito is the art of cutting a recessed design on a plain smooth clay-walled object. The cutting tool is a triangular-shaped cutter with a razor sharp edge. To allow a much easier and smoother cut, the greenware should be leather-hard (moist), or the cutting can chip and eventually ruin the sculpting.

Before cutting, draw your design on the greenware with a lead pencil. If any pencil lines should remain, the porcelain firing will burn them away.

After the drawing is finished, lightly cut along the designed outline. Then carefully slice away the remaining inside area. Make sure not to make too thin a wall and puncture it. If this happens you will have to repour another object and begin all over.

When the cutting work is completed, take a moist brush and lightly brush over the outline edges to smooth and refine areas that may be coarse and rough.

Most sgraffito work produced on porcelain is made for illumination effects; the technique is very effective with lamps and night-lights. In areas where the wall is thicker the light will pass only dimly through the porcelain. The thinner areas will allow brighter light to pass through. Using different variations of thickness you can create a three-dimensional effect. Lamp parts and accessories can be purchased at most ceramic shops.

Another effect that can be very enhancing is china painting the sgraffito work. When the color is fired onto the ware the color becomes translucent. This will allow the light to pass through, creating a beautiful halo of color (see pages 92–112 for china painting).

When doing sgraffito, first draw your design.

Use the sgraffito tool on the outlining area of the design.

Carefully cut out the areas you want recessed. The recessed area will be thinner, so when light passes through the impression will be brighter than the overall lighted piece.

Different textures can be made by leaving different thicknesses, such as the center of this flower design.

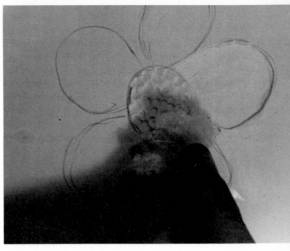

After you have done the sgraffito work, take a brush and lightly wet it down to smooth out the rough-cut areas.

Take a sponge and lightly sponge over the whole design to blend it and to soften all the sharp edges.

PORCELAIN ON PORCELAIN

JASPERWARE SIMULATION

Jasperware is a style of design in which the relief design on an object is done in white against a background of a darker color. Wedgwood, which is a famous brand name of jasperware, is probably familiar to you.

Simulating jasperware (or the Wedgwood look) can be achieved by two different methods. The first is done with a relief design mold. The mold can be a plate, cup, vase, or any object having a plain smooth background with a relief design. You will need a dark-colored porcelain such as green, blue, brown, or black for the background color. You will need white for the relief design.

Make sure your mold is free of dirt and any other porcelain that you may have used in the mold. Wet the design part of the mold with a wet sponge. Soak the whole design area well. This will allow you to paint the design without the porcelain's drying too fast.

Mix a teaspoon of plasticizer with a cup of white porcelain. Mix it thoroughly. This will keep the slip from drying out while using it and prevent a skin from developing on top of the porcelain while it stands open.

After you have mixed the white and sponged the mold, set the mold apart, piece by piece. Set the mold at an angle, positioned like an easel, so it is easier to work.

(53)

Dip a small brush into the white porcelain and outline the design in the mold with the slip. This will allow the inside of the design area to be covered more easily.

After outlining, take a larger brush and slip-paint the whole inside area. Repeat the painting three times, making sure you cover the whole area the same number of times and with the same thickness of paint. If an area is not painted the same, the whiteness will not be white enough when fired because the colored porcelain, which is to be the background, will show through the white.

Work on a small area at a time so you do not forget where and how many times you've painted there.

Paint the mold design on all the mold parts where needed. When that is finished, band the mold tightly for pouring.

Pour the colored slip into the mold and leave it in for the desired thickness (see pages 25–31 for pouring). Then pour out the excess.

Here are two sides of a box impressed with a design for the jasperware technique.

Molds with recessed designs are ideal for the jasperware simulation. There are many molds made specifically for the look of jasperware.

Sponge the mold design so the design is moist. This will allow slip to be applied to the design without its drying too fast while you work with it.

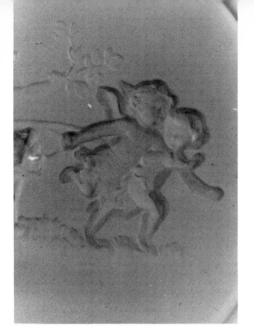

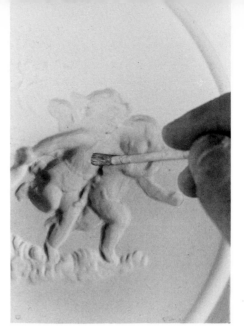

Here you can see how the design was first outlined to make a complete coverage easier without getting out of the line.

After outlining, fill in the whole area inside. Make sure the area coverage is solid and has three complete coats, or the whiteness of the design may have color show through from the colored background.

When it comes out of the mold you will see that the design will be white on a dark background. When fired, the dark color will become darker and the white will stand out beautifully.

The second, and more creative, way is the method for making the original hand-painted jasperware relief. First, pour a smooth object with any deep-colored porcelain. After it is poured, take it out of the mold and let it dry until it is leather-hard (just slightly moist). If you must leave the piece for any length of time, put it into a plastic bag or container to keep it moist.

Once the piece is as dry as you wish, use the same mixture of plasticizer and white porcelain as in the first method.

Set the object at an angle so that you can work easily. You will be following almost the same procedure as with the relief mold except that you are painting an original design on the object.

Draw a design on the object with a lead pencil. Then paint the areas with three coats of white porcelain, to fully cover the design you have drawn.

After the solid coverage is completed you may inscribe with a lace tool or cleaning tool any fine detail work desired.

When the detail is done, take a wet brush and lightly brush over the design. This will make any rough edges smooth and delicate.

Now the piece is ready for the kiln. Firing this type of work in a kiln does not require any special firing. Just fire it with any plain fired objects.

(55)

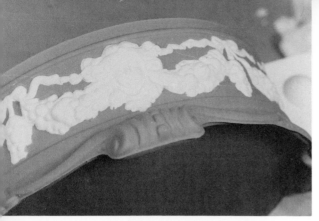

This is the casting after the mold was closed and cast with the colored background slip. You can see the white design against the dark color.

This is the top of the casting, which is the lid to the box.

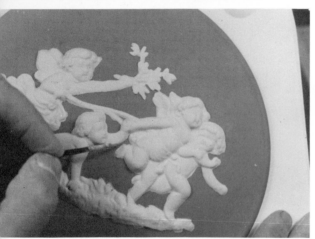

After the casting is taken out of the mold, any mistakes made can be painted over with the same colored slip. Lightly brush over the area where there may be a flaw.

Historical mug done in this technique after being fired. When the piece shrinks in firing the detail becomes much finer.

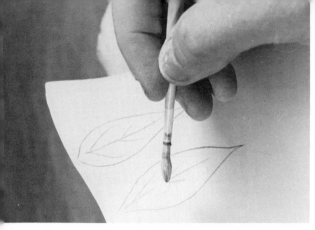

When creating your own jasperware simulation, draw your design first, then coat the designed area solid with slip.

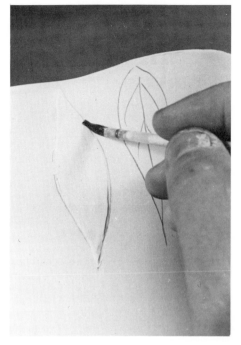

Make sure there are three solid coats to ensure a pure white design. Otherwise the colored slip background will show through, making the white design blotchy.

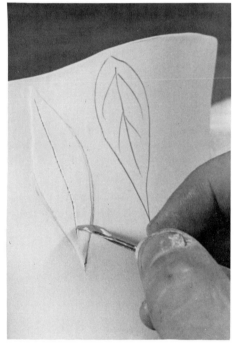

After coverage, use your cleaning tool to incise the detail of the design.

You will have rough edges where the incising was done.

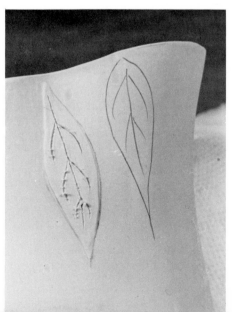

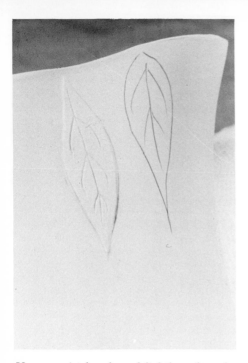

Use a moist brush and lightly soften the edges and detail to make the design smooth and even.

This ginger jar was made with a small leaf design around the top. The lid also has small leaves with beads.

SPONGING

Sponging and textured effects can also be produced. Dip a sponge into slip and lightly dab the slip onto a plain object. Make sure the ware is slightly damp so the slip will adhere to it properly. The sponge will also stick to the object if it is not moist enough for application.

This effect is very nice for background textures of flower-work boxes or other objects requiring texture.

For the sponge technique you need a small container of slip and an elephant-ear sponge.

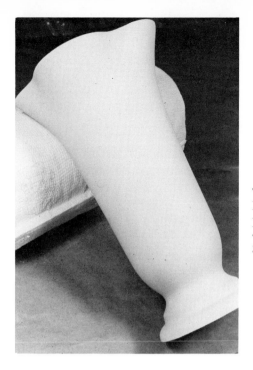

The object you wish to sponge should be leather-hard (slightly moist), to allow application of slip. The object should be rested at an angle so you can work more easily and get an even sponge texture over the piece.

When sponging, dab lightly to prevent getting globs of slip anywhere and to keep the sponge effect even and controlled.

The texture from sponging is great for background effects for many plain items. Here you can see the difference on a piece, part of which has been sponged.

FLOWER MAKING

There are many types of flowers that are made by the hand-forming method. Creating them in porcelain adds another dimension of beauty unlike any other art form.

In order to correctly wedge and shape each piece the plasticity of the porcelain clay must be correct. The plasticity is the moistness of the clay. If not moist enough when shaping, the forms will dry and become cracked.

Tools and cutting shapes are also needed. Numerous types of forms and materials are used to add the many details necessary for the realistic beauty of each petal leaf and complete flower. Metal cutting tools and ceramic press forms are used to cut the desired shapes for the specific flower. Rubber press forms are also used to cut and create the veins throughout the leaves.

MAKING THE CLAY

The most important factor in flower making is the clay and its plasticity. Making the clay yourself is best. If you are using a reputable porcelain slip to cast, this should also be suitable for making your clay.

One way you can make clay is by saving the dried-up slip that is left after cleaning out a poured mold. The excess in the pour-hole gate and the top of the mold can be used if accumulated and kept moist. You also must be sure that no other dirt or foreign matter gets mixed in with the clay when cleaning the mold. Any dirt or lumps will cause the clay to be rough and unusable. Once you have gathered enough scraps, put them into a ball, making sure it is still moist enough to knead together. If the scraps are bone dry they are no good. The accumulation you save should be kept moist. Put it into a plastic bag or container so it is sealed. This will save the clay until you are ready to use it.

If you ever have a whole casting come out wrong and it is still quite moist, save it also. Any remaining scraps are fine so long as they are moist and pliable.

To make larger portions of clay, pick out a large mold that you use for casting. Pour slip into the mold and let the casting become about one-quarter inch thick. Then pour the excess slip out. Leave the casting set in the mold until the glossiness of the slip disappears. This indicates it is dried enough to take out and form in a ball. If you leave it in the mold too long it will become too hard and thus unsuitable to use. Put this also into a container to keep moist until needed.

After you have made a few pounds of clay, you will need to add a bit of plasticizer, depending on the dryness of the clay. This liquid will keep the clay moist while working with it. It will also keep the clay from cracking while shaping and wedging. The mixture should have one tablespoon of plasticizer to one pound of clay.

When forming the flowers always make sure the clay not being used is in a CLOSED compartment. Once it has dried it is very difficult to restore it to the proper plasticity.

Depending on what you are creating, colored porcelains are very effective. If yellow flowers are being made, use a yellow porcelain. This will save your having to paint the white porcelain flower yellow; it will need only shading and detail painting.

When making clay for flower making, save any excess clay from pouring and cleaning molds. Stick the remains of the clay in a plastic bag to keep it moist.

Items cast for flower work should be kept moist so attaching of flowers and leaves can be made. If the pieces are dry, the slip will not adhere correctly; moisture permits adhesion.

Containers such as these can also be used to hold poured greenware until it is ready to use.

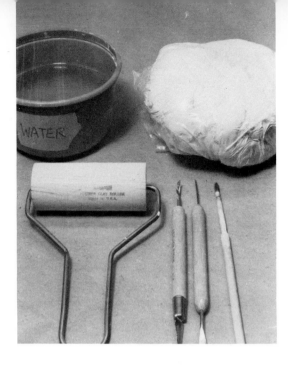

Basic tools for flower making: water, clay roller, double-ended cleaning tool, lace needle tool, brush, and moist clay.

TOOLS

Proper tools will make this venture much more enjoyable and a lot easier; without them, assembling would be very cumbersome. The following tools and accessories are needed to achieve the following flower creations:

1. Lace tool. A long pointed needlelike tool that is also used for lace draping. Here it is used to position centers and vines.

2. Cleaning tool. This should be the tool with a triangular-shaped cutter and a curved cutting end.

3. Clay roller. A rolling tool that rolls out the clay thin for cutting.

4. Sieve or strainer. This is used to create the centers of the flowers, the stamens.

5. Small paint brush. For painting the slip on the parts to be joined together.

6. Paper toweling. To prop or hold up a part that may need shaping so it will not lie flat and lifeless.

7. Clay. Whatever amount and color preferred.

THE CASTING
FOR THE FLOWER ATTACHING

Before deciding on what design you are about to create, it is best to know the shape of the cast ornament. This will determine your flower and how much creative design you will need. If the item to be decorated is small you will want to use a small flower. Thus, the arrangement to be made depends on the size of the object.

Jewel boxes and vases are ideal for flower decorating, and large flat tiles make great practice sheets for new creative designs. All castings should be moist to attach, so they will adhere properly.

The basic form for attaching can be poured in a different color to give contrast to the flowers. This will make the flower design stand out from the colored background. Pastel yellow and blues appear the nicest for contrast. If you do not want to paint the flowers and leaves, the colored ornament will still allow the creation to have a finished colored look. With a white background, the flower creation would just fade into the ornament if it was of the same white porcelain, unless you poured the item in white and did the leaves and flowers in colored clay. It is up to your own imagination as to which color combinations you want to develop to enhance your piece.

PROPPING LIDS OF JEWEL BOXES

If using boxes cast in porcelain for flower arranging, you will have to make sure that you do not attach too much weight to the lid. Try to arrange the flower design according to the size of the box. If too much weight is attached the lid will sag. Use the ceramic fiber, which is discussed on page 41, to stuff the box underneath the lid, supporting it and preventing it from sagging in under the weight of the flowers. The lid must also be fired lying on the box. This will make sure the lid and box fire up evenly; otherwise the lid might fire out of shape. The box works as a setter to allow the lid to shrink at the desired rate.

But, if you recall, anything fired together will be permanently attached. So you will need flint to keep the lid from being fired to the box.

Flint is a powdered substance which, when added to liquid, acts as a separator when firing together two objects that must be separated after the firing. The box and lid are an example. To keep them from sticking together, paint a small coating of the flint on the areas that are to touch each other. Both areas need not be coated; just make sure there is at least a flint separation between two touching areas.

The flint mixture should have two parts of water to one part of flint.

ROLLING OUT CLAY FOR CUTTING

Take out a small amount of clay to be used for cutting the petals and leaves. Do not roll out too much. If you do not work fast enough the rolled-out clay will dry and have to be discarded. A small amount will work well.

Press the small ball of clay in your fingers into a flat pancake and lay it on some paper. This will keep the clay from sticking to the surface when rolling.

After thinning out a small wad of clay, lay it on a small sheet of paper on a flat surface and roll out to your desired thinness; the thinner the clay, the much finer the flowers will become when done.

Take your clay roller and roll the clay about one-eighth inch thick. If you can work with it thinner, all the better. The thinner the cuttings the much finer and more paperlike the flower will become. But it will take time until you get used to it.

After it is rolled out, cut the shapes you will need. After cutting the shapes, put them into an airtight container, resting them on a wet flannel or paper toweling, making sure to keep the container closed at all times. The cuttings need to stay moist so when you are ready to assemble them they are pliable and shapable for the desired arrangement.

When you have cut out all the pieces you will need, you will be ready to start the creative part of flower making.

CREATING A ROSE

To create the rose you will need the rose-cutting kit and the rose-leaf forms.

The rose-petal-cutter kit consists of five different-sized circles, although you use only three of the sizes per flower. Using the three largest circles would make a large rose. The three smallest circles make

CHICKADEE WITH SNOW AND HOLLY. Different molds were incorporated to create the basic structure. Holly, berries, and snow were handcrafted and attached. China painted. Ronald Serfass. Molds by B. J. Mold.

STEIN. China painted. Gold metallic detail and trim. Ronald Serfass. Mold by White Horse Mold.

ABOVE
ELEPHANT CANDLE HOLDER. Basic structure mold poured. Flower and leaves hand formed and attached. China painted. Gold metallic detail and trim. Ronald Serfass. Mold by McNees Molds.

BELOW
HEART BOX. Hand-formed roses and leaves. Unpainted bisque with pink porcelain background. Ronald Serfass. Mold by Schmid Mold.

SONG SPARROW WITH MORNING GLORIES. Basic structure was mold poured. Flowers, vines, and leaves were hand formed and attached. China painted. Ronald Serfass. Molds by B. J. Mold.

BLUE TITS ON DOGWOOD. Eight molds were used to pour all the pieces. Leaves were hand formed. Centers of flowers were made from clay pressed through a strainer. China painted. Ronald Serfass. Molds by B. J. Mold.

JEWEL BOX. Hand-formed rose with leaves. China painted. Ronald Serfass. Mold by Holland Mold.

FLOSSY (LAMB). China painted. Ronald Serfass. Mold by Dushel, not available.

SLATE-COLORED JUNCO. Bird and base mold poured. Holly leaves and berries hand formed and attached. China painted. Ronald Serfass. Mold by Schmid Mold.

CHICKADEE. China painted. Ronald Serfass. Mold by Glenview Molds.

RED FOX. China painted. Ronald Serfass. Mold by White Horse Mold.

MAGNOLIA. China painted. Ronald Serfass. Mold by Jamar Mallory Studio.

CHRISTMAS PLATE. China painted. Gold metallic trim.
Ronald Serfass. Mold by Schmid Molds.

DOGWOOD BRANCH. Two molds were incorporated. Leaves and centers of
flowers were hand formed. China painted. Ronald Serfass. Molds by B. J. Mold.

TOGETHERNESS (GOS-LINGS). China painted. Ronald Serfass. Mold by Holland Mold Co.

SCREECH OWL. Two molds were incorporated for this piece. China painted. Ronald Serfass. Owl mold by Glenview Mold. Pinecones by Duncan Mold Co.

WOOD THRUSH WITH BABIES. Birds, tree branches, and strawberries mold poured. Leaves and work around nest hand-formed and attached. China painted. Ronald Serfass. Molds by B. J. Mold. Strawberries by Duncan Mold.

HIBISCUS WITH BUTTERFLY. China painted. Ronald Serfass. Mold by Jamar Mallory Studio. Butterfly addition by Duncan Mold Co.

SQUIRREL. China painted. Ronald Serfass. Mold by White Horse Mold.

STANDING SWAN. Sponged texture on swan for feathery effect. China painted. Ronald Serfass. Mold by White Horse Mold.

the smallest rose. The three largest circles are the ones we are going to use for this creation.

Cut out six of the largest circles, five of the next largest, and four of the next size, thus creating six large, five medium, and four small circles. Put these cuttings into a wet flannel-lined container to keep them moist.

Take one at a time and thin the upper edges of the circle with your fingers, leaving the bottom edge a little thicker for attaching. Take the wooden end of a tool or use your thumb and cup the circles, transforming them into cupped petals.

Do this to all six large petals and attach them with a small dab of slip to the casting being used. Assemble them in a circle.

Take the next five circles and wedge them also, thinning the edges. Cup them in the same way and attach them inside the six larger petals. When assembling, prop the petals with paper toweling to hold the shape of the flower till dry.

Take the last four circles and work them the same as above. Attach them inside the five petals. Then take out the paper toweling when the clay is dry enough to stand by itself.

After you have all the petals positioned, take a small wad of clay and press it through the strainer. This will make a beautiful cluster of stamens for the center.

Take the lace tool and with it place the stamens so they are evenly spread around the center.

Cut out the shapes of the leaves with the rose press form. These are made of rubber and have the vein impressions on them. They come in different sizes. After you have cut out the various sizes you want, serrate the edges like a rose leaf's. You can use the rounded edge of a daisy cutter (which can also be purchased where the rose cutters were) to evenly serrate the edges.

Take the rubber press forms and lay them over the cut leaves, pressing to create the fine veins. Place the leaves where your design calls for them and prop them with paper toweling until they dry in position.

For those of you who would like a small bud, take a small circle and roll it in your fingers. Then take another small circle and roll that over the first roll. This will create a small partially opened bud. Also cut two leaves to attach to the bud.

To attach this to the larger flower, roll out some clay into a vine-type stem and run it from the large flower to the area where you want the bud. Attach a few smaller leaves around the stem to finish off the design.

Any other leaves needed should be added to balance out the arrangement.

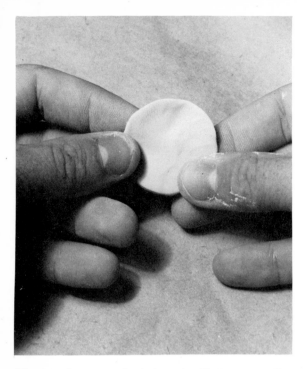

The rose flower needs circles cut with the rose cutter kit. Thin out the edges of the circles and smooth out the whole petal.

Using the fat end of a tool, run the handle over the center of the circle to "cup" the petal.

Apply slip to the bottom part of the petal and attach to the piece to be decorated. Curl back the end of each petal when attached so it has a slight curl, like a rose petal. Put some paper toweling under the back of each petal to keep it propped up as it dries.

Attach the second one the same way, propping up the edge till dried.

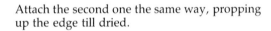

Six petals should be attached in a circle, still using paper toweling to hold them in place.

The next circle has five petals, which are slightly smaller. They are attached and positioned in a circle inside the first six. Prop them also with toweling.

Four smaller petals are attached inside the five petals. After all the petals are attached and dry, carefully remove the paper toweling, making sure not to damage anything.

The center stamens are made by pressing moist clay through a strainer.

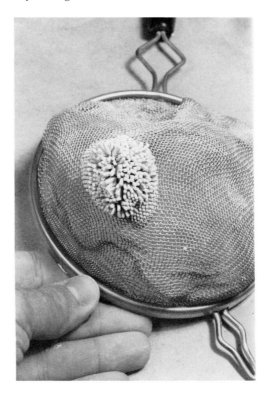

Cut off the stamens and attach them with slip to the center of the flower. Using the lace needle tool, press on the stamens and position them in a circular area.

Cut the leaf shapes and, with a daisy cutter, serrate the edges to simulate rose leaves.

Using the rubber leaf impression form for rose leaves, press over the cut leaf and create the veins.

Attach the leaves with slip and position them under the flower petals. Prop the leaves so they have lifelike curves and curls.

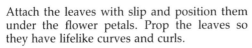

The finished rose with leaves.

Roll a few more circles around the first one, creating a small rosebud.

To form a rosebud, take a small circle and roll it in your finger to form a center for the bud.

Cut a few small thin leaves and attach them to the bottom end of the small bud.

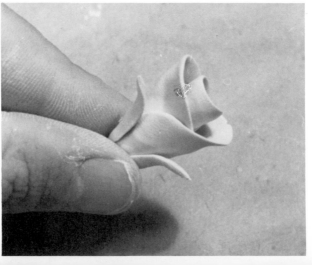

(69)

VIOLETS

The medium teardrop cutter is used to cut the shapes for the violet flower. Be sure to keep them in an airtight container on some wet flannel or paper toweling. They must be kept moist for proper shaping.

One at a time, take a teardrop cutting and press the edges thin, making sure the overall texture is smooth. Lay the petal in your palm and inscribe a few random lines on the petal, starting from the pointed end to the rounded edge. This is done with a lace tool (needle end). As you pull from the pointed end, gradually lighten your pressure so the line fades out toward the end. Use a wet brush and lightly brush over the lines to make sure they are smooth. Do this to all the petals.

Attach the first petal with a little slip on the pointed end. When positioning, keep the petal end formed upward so it does not lie flat.

Attach the next two petals the same way, positioning them on each side of the first one. The next two petals are attached on the bottom of the last two petals. Make sure they are not lying flat. You want an impression of a little movement in the flowers.

The violet flower has three stamens in the center. Roll out three quarter-inch rolls of clay, with both ends pointed. Using the lace tool, stick it into one of the stamens made, then dip it into some slip for attaching. Press it onto the center of the flower at an angle. Then place the second opposite the first and the third in the center.

After they are all attached and positioned, cover the stamens with slip to cover the small holes made by the lace tool.

Roll out some clay and cut out violet-plant-shaped leaves, following the pattern of the violet press forms. Press the veins after cutting and position the leaves according to the object and design you are producing. (See photo on page 119 for ginger jar decorated with violets.)

This is a lid to a powder box and is ideal for flower creating. Make sure the piece is moist so attaching is successful.

The petals of the violet flower are made with the teardrop cutter. Use a lace tool to incise the lines on the petals from the pointed to the rounded end.

Attach the first petal with slip.

Attach two more petals, one on each side of the first, pulling the ends up slightly for shape.

Attach the lower two in the same way, lifting the ends.

Roll a small tube shape and attach it to the center with a lace needle tool.

Attach the other two centers alongside the first.

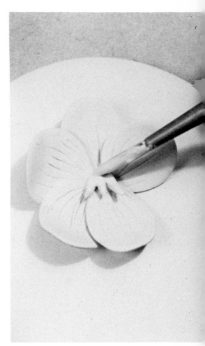

Apply some slip over the centers to cover the holes from the lace tool.

Using a violet leaf press form, cut leaves and attach them according to your design.

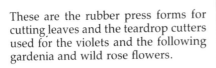

The assembled violets with leaves.

These are the rubber press forms for cutting leaves and the teardrop cutters used for the violets and the following gardenia and wild rose flowers.

GARDENIA FLOWER

There are three sizes of teardrop cutters that can be used to cut the gardenia petals, but it is best to use the medium cutters for the average-size flower.

The leaf shapes are all four different sizes and can be used according to what size flower and object you are decorating.

Using a small wad of clay, take the clay roller and roll the clay out flat. Cut out about twenty teardrops with the large cutter and store them in an airtight container.

For the gardenia arrangement, a rounded box and lid are very good. Make sure the object being decorated is kept moist, so the flowers adhere when attached.

Take one petal and press the edges so they are thin, flat, and smooth. Press the pointed end together so it shapes the petal. Treat each petal in this way, then paint some slip on the underside of each petal before attaching it to the lid of the box. Assemble six of these in a circle slightly apart. Add six more the same way in the spaces between the first six.

The next four petals must be cupped so they are proper for the center enclosure. Take a handle of a tool, or use your thumb, and pull over the petal from the rounded end to the point. This will make the petal form a cup shape. Attach four of these in the center, far enough apart so four more can be put in the center of them.

For the center, take a teardrop shape and press it out thin. Then roll it up to form a center enclosure. Cut the end off to shorten it and press it into the center of the flower with some slip.

Cut the gardenia leaves in various sizes. Press the veins into them and keep them in a moist container till ready to use.

Attach the leaves wherever your design allows. To hold up the leaves while soft, prop them underneath with paper towels. This will make it possible for you to shape and turn the leaves any way and to hold them in that position till they are dry. Afterward you can take away the paper-towel stuffing.

A bud is made with four petals shaped together around a center, as with the full-blown flower.

The vine is a small wad of clay rolled out thin enough to form a rounded curvature to follow the shape of the box lid. If the vine material dries out fast, add a little plasticizer to it, reroll, and reposition it on the lid. When attaching the vine, paint slip only on the ends where the attachment is made. This will allow for shrinkage between the two joining areas.

When the vine is attached, add the remaining leaves. If you want to add a closed bud, take a small wad of clay and twist it in your fingers to form a pointed, twisted gardenia bud. The final creation depends on your imagination and the object you are decorating.

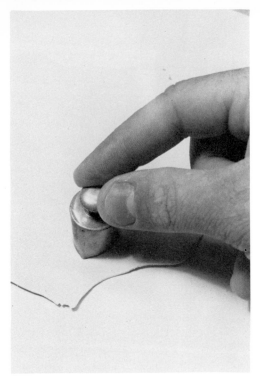

By pressing into the rolled-out clay the gardenia petals are cut.

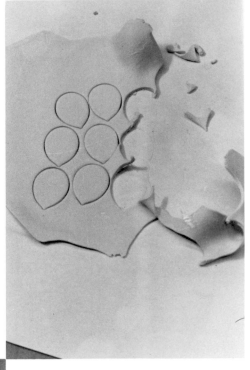

Cut as many shapes as you can out of the clay rolled to avoid wasting the clay.

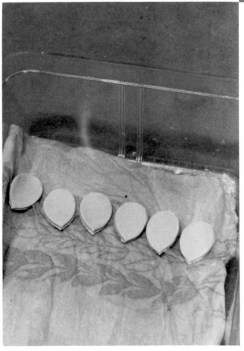

Keep them in a moist damp box until you are ready for them.

Cut leaves should also be stored in the damp box until you press veins on them.

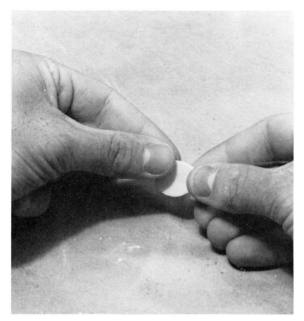

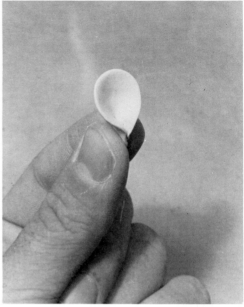

Take each petal and wedge its edges so they are thin.

Press the pointed end together so the petal becomes cupped.

Apply slip to the pointed end for attaching.

Press the pointed end onto the piece, cupped part down. Pull the rounded end up slightly so it has a bit of height.

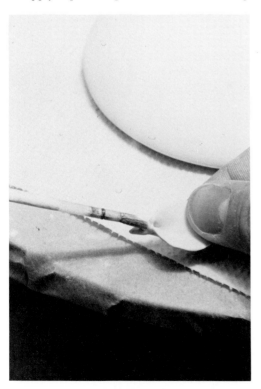

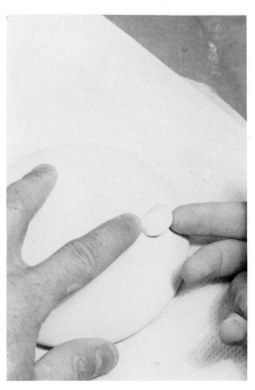

(75)

Apply six petals in a circle evenly spread apart.

Apply another six between the spaces of the first six. Make sure you keep them evenly spaced apart with the ends raised.

For the next four petals, cup them as you did for the roses.

Attach these evenly in the center of the last six.

Apply the last four the same way.

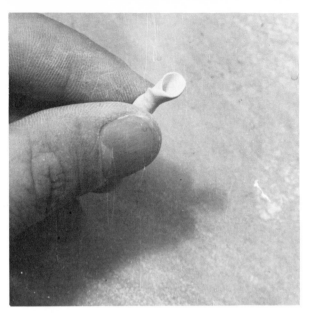

The center of the gardenia is made by rolling a teardrop with your finger.

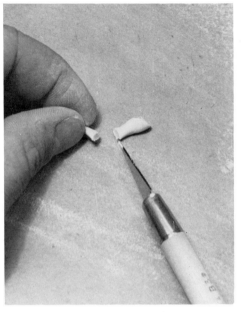

Cut the end off to shorten it. The center should be lower than the rest of the flower.

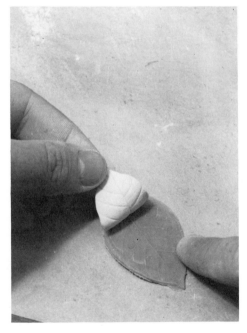

Press the gardenia leaf press forms over the cut leaves to give them veins.

Attach the leaves in the same way that the petals were attached. Prop the leaves with some paper toweling to give them shape and curl.

Make a vine by rolling some moist clay, and run it gracefully from the main flower to the bottom of the box. With slip attach the vine only on the ends and in the center, and make sure you leave enough slack between each attachment so shrinking can occur without cracking. After the vine is applied, add the smaller leaves according to the vine's curvature.

A smaller gardenia bud can be made by forming four small petals together with a small center.

The assembled gardenia with leaves, finished with china paint.

WILD ROSE

Roll out some clay and cut out five of the large teardrop shapes. Take each petal shape and thin the edges as you did for all the other flowers, cupping each petal in the same way as for the gardenia. Do this to all five petals.

Position them in a circle. Press some clay through a strainer in the same way that the rose stamens were made. Cut off the sievings and position them inside the center of the petals. Make sure enough slip is painted on the center to hold the stamens.

Pull the stamens apart with a lace or needle tool so there is a slight opening in the center to hold a small berry. Roll a small ball and attach it to the center of the flower in the midst of the stamens. Then take your cleaning tool and press a small indentation in the berry.

The leaves for this wild rose are of the same shape as those for the cultivated rose except they do not have serrated edges. These are left plain.

This flower is made on a vase in a later project (pages 130–134), showing an arrangement and design.

Petals for the wild rose are cut with the large teardrop cutter. Then they are cupped and attached, the five petals overlapping slightly.

Press some clay through a strainer to make the stamens. Using a lace needle tool, apply this to the center of the petals and spread open the center.

Roll out a small ball of clay and attach it to the space in the center of the stamens. Press a small indentation in the center of the ball with a tool.

The assembled wild rose with leaves.

LACE DRAPING

One of the most delicate and intricate techniques in porcelain making is lace draping. This art has been practiced through the ages, and examples have found their way into many fine collections in museums and antique shops throughout the world.

If you have ever seen any of the figurines of women with frilly lace-draped dresses and skirts, you will realize the work involved in planning a lace draping.

A twist of the lace can make the difference between a lifelike portrayal and a stiff mannequin.

The movement of the figurine body decides the flowing movement of the garment that is to be worn. If the basic body shape is plain and stiff, the lace draping can only be the same.

If a leg or arm is raised or turned, the lace will be formed in position, creating a much lovelier feel and look. Try to pick out figurines that will provide a more extravagant design. However, it is best to begin with something a little easier at first.

There are many mold companies that carry the forms for lace draping, some with arms raised, legs bent, heads turned, and assuming many other positions. It depends upon what you are looking for. Remember, as you progress, be daring and try the more elaborate laces and drapings. You will never regret it.

Use Proper Lace. The lace used to make the porcelain lace must be all cotton. To make you understand why, I must tell you what happens to a lace-draped article when it is fired.

Once the object is porcelain lace-draped, the cotton material draping, when fired, burns away, leaving the thin porcelain film of the lace impression. If the lace had any polyester in it, the fabric would melt as the heat burned it, causing the porcelain to droop and run together, disfiguring the object.

Remember that cotton lace is essential in lace draping. Once it is fired, you will think that it is still the lace material, but it is really the porcelain that is left, creating the lace design.

BALLERINA

I picked the ballerina for the lace-draping project because it has nice movement and the lace draping itself is simple enough to learn easily.

When pouring the body parts, pour them moderately thin so there is not too much weight stress on the base. But pour the base a little heavier so it can hold the weight put on it.

Pour the body parts in flesh porcelain and the flat base in white, or whatever color you prefer. After you have poured all the parts, put holes in the arms and leg parts for ventilation where attachments are made.

(81)

Clean all seam lines on parts, making sure the areas are sponged smooth and clean. Before doing any attaching, stuff the base's underside with the ceramic fiber (see page 41). This packing will help support the weight of the figure so the base does not sag.

Lace can be bought in many different designs and densities. Just make sure that it is 100 percent cotton. The lace I am using has a flowered design with a fluted edge, but any design can be used. Make sure there is enough lace density over the design area so when fired there is enough porcelain to withstand the glazing later on.

Cutting the lace to the proper length is important. The lace should be about one-half inch longer than needed so you can overlap the ends. You will need a piece long enough to go around the waist and bosom. You will also need two more lengths of lace for the ballerina tutu, one for the lift underneath and one for the top dress part. The dress part can be anywhere from twelve to fifteen inches long, depending on how ruffly you want the dress to be. The lace underneath should be cut slightly more narrow so it does not show longer than the top dress.

After you have cut the dress part, sew across the waistline part and pull it together to create the ruffly effect. This will make it much easier for draping.

Before doing any lace draping, you should attach the legs. Make sure you join them with the flesh porcelain slip; otherwise you will have discolored joints (see pages 32–38 for stick-ons).

Take the body and position it onto the base so the toe is pointing over the edge of the narrow end of the base. The slip you want to use for the dipping of the lace should be mixed with a little water so it is not thick and gooey. You can put it into a cup or a large dish depending on how much work you are doing. The container must be large enough to dip the lace in completely.

Dip the waist-part lace into the porcelain and saturate it fully. Then take it out and pull your fingers across the length to take away the excess so the lace design is visible. Make sure the fancy hole design is clear and sharp.

Take the lace, lay it in your palm, and pat it lightly. This will take the slip that may have remained out of the holes.

Take the lace and drape it around the waist and bosom, pulling it around the back so it overlaps. Make sure there are no loose ends, and that the overlapping is secure. If the lace is not overlapped, when it is fired the resulting shrinkage could leave an opening in the lace.

When draping, make sure you do not leave any drip marks on the figure. When fired, the white porcelain slip used for dipping will show up on the body.

Dip the short-length lace for underneath the tutu. Then follow the same procedure as with the waist, making sure all the holes are clear of porcelain. Take this lace and drape it around the waist, making sure you do not touch the leg parts too much. Any excess slip on the legs will have to be cleaned off.

Take your lace tool, using the large thick end, and lightly press the lace into the waist area. If it is a little dry you may add a little slip for better adherence. After the waist area is joined, use the lace tool to pull up the ends of the tutu. This will give it the lift and airiness that it needs.

Take the second lace material and follow the same process, draping it onto the waist over the first draping. Pull up on the dress again so the part at the leg is raised a little from the kneee.

To finish the dress, I took small lace flowers and dipped them in the white porcelain and wrapped them around the waist. This hid the joinings of the dress and waist perfectly.

I also took two flowers for a small headpiece. After the draping is finished, make sure you put some ceramic fiber under the arms to prevent any drooping.

It will be best to put the figure aside so no one will touch it because it is a very fragile piece.

The firing of this piece is a slow procedure. The joints and lace need slow firing so the lace and moisture evaporate gradually. The piece should be given extended firing at a low temperature.

Lace draping materials: flesh slip for assembling the figure, white slip for dipping the lace, plasticizer for mixing with slip if needed, brush for applying slip, and a lace needle tool for applying lace.

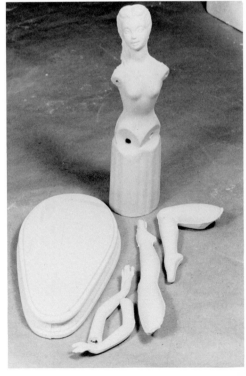

The ballerina used for this demonstration has these stick-on parts. Make sure there are holes in the sections where the arms and legs join the body.

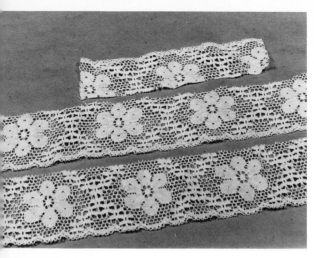

The lace can have any design but must be 100 percent cotton. Other lace will not be suitable.

The base on which the ballerina is to rest should be stuffed underneath with ceramic fiber to support the weight of the ballerina; otherwise the base will sag from stress.

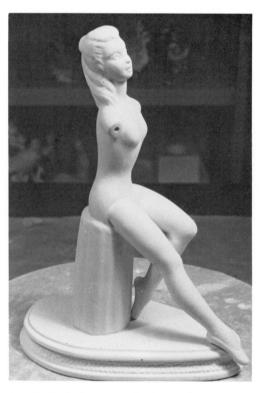

Attach the ballerina to the base, then slip on the two legs.

Dip the small section of lace cut for the breast and waist into the white slip making sure it is saturated all over.

With your fingers press over the lace so the holes become unclogged. The lace design must be clean and sharp.

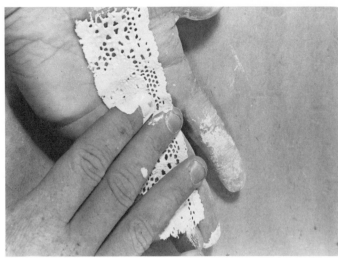

Pat the lace over your palm to release any excess slip that may accumulate while dipping. You can also lay it on some paper and pat it so it is evenly covered and not globbed.

Wrap the dipped lace around the waist and chest area, making sure there is enough room for attaching the arms.

The back lace part should be overlapped enough so that when it is fired the lace stays together.

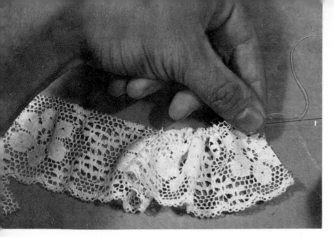

The lace for the tutu can be sewn on a machine to gather the lace so that it is frilly. By pulling on the end thread you can make the lace as full as you like before dipping.

Dip the lace and pat again so the holes are cleared for clean, sharp detail.

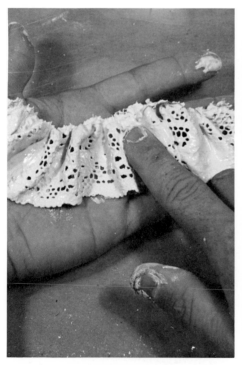

Spread out the gathered lace so excessive slip can be removed. If too much is left it will cause the lace to look globby and unattractive. You want it to have a delicate look.

Wrap the tutu lace part around the waist, making sure you do not get any white slip on the flesh-poured body. If you do, make sure you clean it off or it will show up as two colors when high-fired.

With the lace tool's larger end press in the lace at the waist area so it is completely attached. Make sure it is fully joined to the top of the dress.

Lift the tutu with the lace tool so the lace is light and airy.

After you have wrapped the second dress part over the first, dip a small piece of flowered lace and wrap it around the waist to cover up the joining of the upper lace and the tutu.

Attach the arms after all lace draping is completed. The arms are very graceful, so take care that they are attached correctly. The head decoration is also cut from the same flowered lace that supplied the waist decoration. Attach it to the hair with slip.

Attachment of head piece.

The stretched-out arms will need some ceramic fiber propped under them to prevent their sagging during firing.

The completed ballerina.

GLAZING THE BALLERINA AFTER PORCELAIN FIRING

After the porcelain firing is completed, and the kiln has been given the required cooling time, remove the piece from the kiln and take out the ceramic fiber from under the arms and base. When removing the fiber, be very careful cleaning off the lace. It is very fragile until it has been glazed and refired.

Add a small amount of water to some clear glaze. The glaze can be a high-fire glaze (cone 2) or a regular glaze (cone 06), whichever is preferred. Lightly brush the glaze over the dress part. Put on two light coats, making sure you get underneath the lace. This glazing will give the lacing much more strength. After the glazing is done, fire the piece again. Propping is not required in this glaze firing since the temperature does not reach the porcelain firing, which would cause sagging.

DECORATING

After the glaze firing, you are ready for the color additions and final steps. It is best to work on the facial features first—lips, eyes, and then the hair (see china painting). Make sure the colors are soft and subtle. Since flesh porcelain was used, there is no need to paint the flesh areas of the body.

The shoes can be colored to coordinate with the dress. The dress is decorated with a pearl essence lustre. This creates a beautiful brilliant glow. It can be bought in many different colors. (For application, see coloring, pages 112, 113.)

All these color applications can be fired at the same time and cone 018 or 017 is the required cone. It is usually called a gold-firing temperature.

3

COLORING

OVERGLAZES

The most popular overglazes are china paints, metallics, lustres, and decals. These all need special care and handling to ensure proper results.

Overglaze means exactly what the word implies. The substance must go over the object that has been through a glaze firing. The outcome and finish of the overglaze depends on the glaze finish, so make sure you are not wasting your time on a badly glazed piece. China paints can also be painted on porcelain that has not been glazed, although china paints are also called overglazes.

Overglazing high-gloss glazes will give a brighter finish; satin gloss will give a duller finish.

All overglazes must be used on completely cleaned and dust-free ware. No water (except for the decals) should be used with these overglazes.

(91)

CHINA PAINTS

China paints have been used for many years throughout the world. Most of the colors used today for china-painting are still the powdered colors hand-mixed by the user.

The only colors I use are the powdered ones. The premixed colors are usually quite oily so they do not dry out so soon, but when they are used for painting the oiliness keeps the colors from drying, making handling of the piece very difficult. Usually the only way they will dry will be in the china-paint firing. This makes painting the piece much more tedious. To properly paint, one must fire many times in order to add the different colors needed to finish the piece. These firings cost money. As I want to keep costs down to a minimum, I use the powdered colors.

After learning to use the powdered colors, and by following my technique, coloring can be done in one firing. Using the powder, turpentine, and oil, the paints can be mixed to reach the proper consistency that will allow the applications to dry rapidly. This permits all colors to be applied in one firing and is less time-consuming.

In painting birds, animals, and flowers, both matt and gloss colors are needed. Matt colors are the most widely preferred, since they give the desired realistic finish. Gloss colors are used mainly for eyes and glossy foliage. By intermixing gloss and matt colors you can also create a satin finish, sometimes needed for specific items.

My favorites are nineteen matt colors and six gloss colors. The list is as follows:

MATT COLORS		GLOSS COLORS
Chestnut brown	Steel gray	Ebony black
Paris brown	Shell pink	Finishing brown
Chocolate brown	American beauty rose	Foliage green
Black	Flesh red	Cherry red
Jasper blue	Pompadour red	Chartreuse green
Robin's-egg blue	Poppy red	Orange peel
Yellow brown	Terra-cotta	
Dark yellow	Violet	
Golden yellow	Flux for matt colors	
Grass green		

These colors, intermixed, can create new colors without having to buy more. There are only two colors that will not mix—the reds and the yellows. The yellow, when mixed with any red, will always fire up yellow since the yellow eats and overpowers the red. The other colors cause no problems.

PREPARING POWDERED COLORS FOR PAINTING

You will need a palette, a palette knife, oil of copaiba, and odor-free thinner or turpentine. Using odor-free thinner will keep the smells out of the air.

Small amounts of color should be put on the palette at a time. The powder colors go a long way, so be sparing with them. Even half a teaspoonful will be enough for most amounts needed. Add the thinner to the powder color with an eye dropper or the palette knife. Add just enough to make the powder into a thick dry paste. Make sure all the powder is thoroughly mixed so no particles of color are left dry. If the color has not been mixed smoothly and evenly when it is applied, the firing may cause spots to occur from the dried powder.

After mixing the powder with thinner, take a small amount of oil of copaiba and mix together till smooth. The consistency should not be runny. If the color dries on the palette too soon you know you need more oil, which will keep the color from drying too fast. The more oil you add the longer the color will stay open (wet) for your application and blending.

When applied to the porcelain the mixture should stay moist long enough to permit smoothing and blending. If not, streaks and blotches will occur. However, if the color stays wet and seems never to want to dry, you have added too much oil and must add a bit of the powder color to make it drier. Through practice and experimenting you will soon learn to make the mix you want. But don't get frustrated—remember the discipline needed to withstand the trials and triumph over the errors as you perfect this fine art.

After the colors that you will need are mixed, try to keep them in one area to prevent their drying out too fast.

USING FLUX WITH YOUR MATT COLORS

For certain items that are being painted you may want a satin finish. By mixing a small amount of flux, you will make that certain color mixed with it have a slight sheen. The more you mix with the color the glossier it will get.

It is this substance that makes the gloss colors glossy. This is mixed in exactly the same way the other colors are.

BRUSHES FOR CHINA-PAINTING

I use two kinds of brushes in my painting—the shaders and the stipplers.

The shaders are soft-haired and come square shaped, round mop

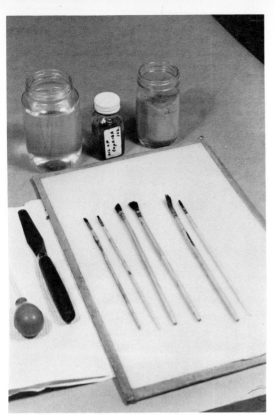

Materials for china-painting: turpentine or odor-free thinner, oil of copaiba, powdered china colors, eye-dropper, palette knife, glass palette, pointed and square shader brushes, stippler brushes, and paper toweling.

The first step in mixing the china-paint color is to mix the turpentine or odor-free thinner into the powder. Using an eyedropper will make it easier to add small amounts at a time.

Using the palette knife, grind down the powder with the turpentine into a thick paste. Make sure all the powder is mixed so there are no powder specks left.

With the palette knife gradually add oil of copaiba to the dry paste mixture. Use just enough oil to give the color its moistness. The color must stay wet while it is being applied; if not enough oil is mixed into the color the paint will dry too fast.

The color when completely mixed should have a glossy sheen and should be kept in a small area to prevent it from drying too fast when setting.

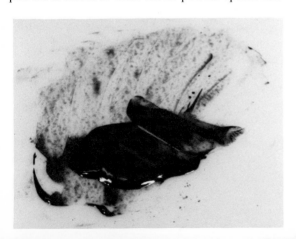

shaped, and pointed. They are used mainly to add the color over the areas that are to be painted and smoothed.

The stipplers are much denser, with many more hairs. They have a flat edge, which is used to drag and stipple color smooth. Without these stipplers the color would be very hard to keep streakless and without blotches. The stipplers are also used to blend two or more colors together, making colors blend from one to the other beautifully. The softening of the hard edges of color is done with the stippler also.

CHINA-PAINTING METHOD

When china-painting, remember to always have your color mixed with enough oil so it does not dry too soon. It must stay wet long enough to blend well.

Apply the prepared color with a shader brush, dabbing the color at random over the desired area. Do not apply more color than needed because you will have to remove the excess, so only dab on the color and keep the application light.

Take a large stippler and drag it over the dabs, pulling the color together to spread over and completely cover the area. If the color dries before you are able to smooth it, you need more oil of copaiba. This will keep it open (wet).

When smoothing out a one-color coverage, use the largest stippler you can so there will be fewer brushstrokes.

When dragging the color, pull over the application lightly. This will allow the color to flow evenly, and strokes and blotches will be less prevalent.

When you wish to use two colors for blending, apply both the colors where needed. Then take the stippler and pull the colors together, overlapping them. This should create a slight color mix. Slowly begin to soften the joinings by pulling the stippler over each color (dragging). After the colors are blended the gradation from one color to the next should be subtle.

There are basically two ways of smoothing out color with the stipplers. The one must used is called "dragging," which is done by pulling the brush lightly over the color, to smooth out and pull colors together. The other method used to smooth out color with stipplers is called "pouncing" (lifting the brush up and down, touching the color). This creates a fuzzy effect and also blends the colors. Both these methods are used throughout the procedures in this book.

When the china-paint color dries it is inadvisable to go back over it because the turpentine and the oil in the color will soften the first dried color, making it difficult to blend and correct. So remember to apply color and smooth it out as soon as possible. Once it is dried, try not to go back and work it over again.

When applying colors, use a pointed shader or a square shader. Do not apply the color heavily or thickly because the application should be transparent. To blend two colors together, first apply them next to each other as smoothly as possible.

After the color is applied, use a large stippler brush and drag the colors into each other up and down.

Pull the two colors into each other so there is a mixture of both colors.

Take the stippler and drag sideways, making the two colors blend softly from one to the other. Make sure that all streaks and blotches are gone so the colors are perfectly blended.

After the stippling and dragging, the colors should look like this. Blending should be done when color is still slightly wet or you will have trouble smoothing out the color.

Stippling can also be done to china colors. It blends the color but leaves fuzzy effects throughout the color. The stippling effect is done by lifting the brush up and down on the color.

Once color is applied and an area needs to be white again, take a small stippler or the size desired for the area working, and moisten it with the turpentine or thinner, making sure it is just slightly damp. If too much turpentine is used the turpentine will spread all over the color already painted, causing the color to run. You want the brush only slightly damp.

The area you want white you drag and pull over the space you want to clean. This will pull the color off the piece and allow the white porcelain to show through. After each pulling of color wipe the brush on a paper towel. This will allow you to clean the porcelain to a pure white.

Painting on the bisque porcelain (unglazed) is the most widely preferred. It takes the paint much better even though the porcelain is vitreous.

Because the porcelain is nonporous that is all the more reason to drag the color smooth, since the color does not seep into the ware. So laying on the color smoothly is very important.

When working on glazed ware the paint slides much more and the streaks and marks are much harder to smooth out. It takes practice to paint without leaving streaks and lines.

The turpentine or odor-free thinner is used to clean your brushes. Always make sure the colors you have used are washed out of the brush because if the paint is not removed it will get hard and ruin your brush. This happens to almost any brush, so if you do not wish to buy new brushes constantly treat your brushes correctly.

(97)

STEP-BY-STEP PROCEDURES FOR PORCELAIN-PAINTING TECHNIQUES

When applying color to large areas, outline the area to be painted and then dab color throughout the area. The larger the brush used, the less brushing will be needed.

The following steps showing the painting of the sea gull will demonstrate the painting techniques used for porcelain.

For the size area being painted, use the preferred size brush needed for convenience. Drag the stippler over the color till smooth and streakless. Dragging is pulling the color in one direction with the flat edge of the stippler.

(98)

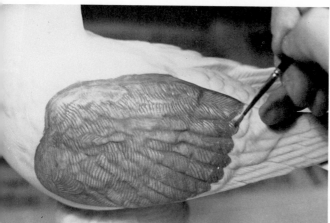

On an area that needs to be white let the clean white porcelain show. I never use white paint because the porcelain white is more beautiful. Here you can see the small detail brush being used to paint the color, leaving the white tips of the wings blank.

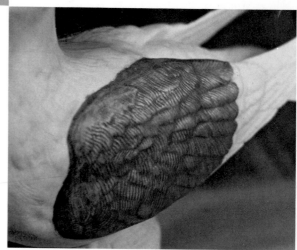

A smooth, even coverage can be easily obtained if the paint is dragged lightly with the stippler. Always remember to use the largest shader or stippler suitable for the area you are painting.

Edges of color should be softened so that the area does not look as if it had been pasted on. Almost all areas of color on birds or animals should be softened unless the area of the color needs to be sharp and distinct.

When applying black areas of color, make the color deep and solid. This is achieved by keeping the color dry and less oily. Here the wing detail is being painted, leaving the white tips blank so the porcelain will show.

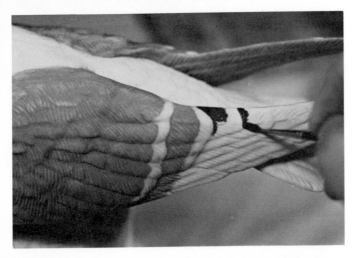

When white areas are wanted, it is best to paint around them and to fill in the solid area.

When all the detail black is painted in, use a small stippler to soften the areas.

When painting birds or animals always paint both sides simultaneously so the colors are identical. Remember to mix enough color for your purpose. If you mix colors together for a certain color or hue, make sure you don't run out of them before you are finished.

(100)

The area on the bird's back has been painted but has a sharp edge. It looks artificial.

Using a stippler, blend the colors with a bit of turpentine. But do not use too much—just make sure the brush is slightly damp. Too much turpentine will make the color spread.

Here the tail area is being smoothed out, a bit of detail being added by dragging some darker color over the textured part.

After the undercolor is applied and smoothed out, you want to add some depth and shadowing. This is what makes any piece realistic and lifelike. Any areas where feathers or fur overlap should have added depth. Here you can see the application of a deeper color around the areas where the wings lie over each other.

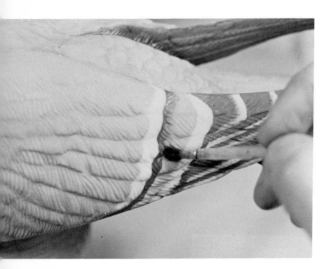

Using a stippler, drag the color outward, blending it into the undercolor.

Make sure all shadings are done with a gradual fading from dark to light.

You can see the difference from the softening and the sharp edge.

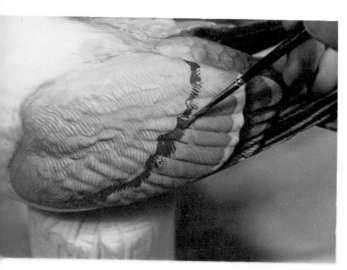

Throughout these pictures you can see the added color and softening for shaded and detail areas.

After the colors on the wings have been softened, add detail by giving highlights to the painted area. Drag your fingers over the colored area, rubbing lightly over the textured area. This will cause the color to lighten and add a highlight.

You can see how the detail and highlights give the piece more depth.

Adding shading around open areas will also make the part of the body seem attached to the basic form. Here I am adding shading around the wing to make it look more attached to the body.

Soften the added color again, making the detail more realistic.

(104)

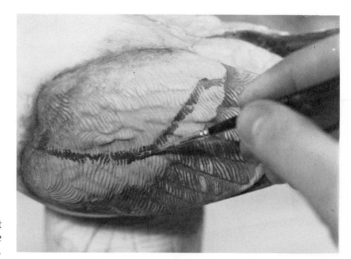

Do shading on all parts that have underlying areas to give them depth and definition. Always make sure all shading is softened and gradually faded from light to dark.

(105)

When painting eyes on a piece, use glossy colors. And the color must be dryer and less oily so the application can be heavier to give it more gloss. Adding flux to any matt color will make the color glossy, but it is better to use a glossy prepared powder. I use the gloss finishing brown and gloss black unless I need a yellow, to which I add flux when it is needed for shininess. Here I am applying the overall color on the eye.

Using a stippler, I smooth out any thick areas that are too heavy because too heavy an application can cause the color to run.

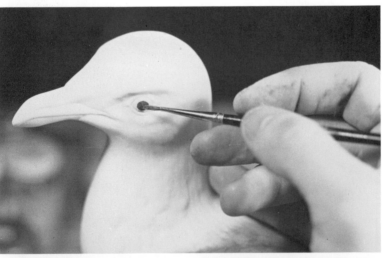

When the undercoat has been applied, paint in the black part of the iris.

After that, take a small detail brush moistened with turpentine and pull the color away from the eyeball to create a highlight and dispel the starey look.

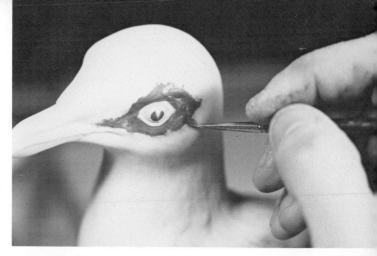

Around the eyes of birds and animals it is good to add a bit of shading to enhance them and make them realistic. Here I dabbed the color around the eyes.

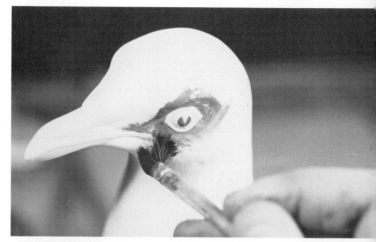

Use a stippler again to soften the area around the eyes and fade the color gradually into the white.

Make sure the whole area is softly blended.

Beaks of birds require a solid color. Drag again with a stippler to make the beak smooth and streakless. Noses on animals are painted the same way, but are usually dark in color.

Added detail is supplied around beaks and noses by adding a deeper shade of color. Add a line of deeper color to the beak opening to define the separation.

To make a beak or nose look attached to the head, dab some color around the joining area.

Then soften with a stippler. This will make the beak look attached and not stuck on.

When painting wood or branches, color should be dabbed on. Large areas need not be covered solid since you drag the color over the area to cover it completely. After the color is smoothed out, take your finger and add highlight as was done on the wings.

When the piece is finished you can see how the added detail and shading contribute to its realism. The steps shown throughout the sea gull painting are the usual applications and softening and blending techniques. The most essential thing to remember is always to keep your color as smooth and soft as possible.

For pieces with foliage I always use grass green matt and chartreuse green gloss. The chartreuse gloss adds the highlight needed to give the leaves life. Here I am adding the chartreuse gloss to the already painted green.

Using the stippler, blend the two colors together so there is no harsh division of color. You want the leaves to look as if sunshine is reflecting off them. These colors will create that illusion.

METALLIC OVERGLAZES

The most widely used metallics are gold and silver, and each is applied to cover with one coat. It should be evenly applied and heavy enough to look a dark brown, not yellow, before firing.

When applied the coverage will look streaky, but when fired it will become opaque and smooth. The items being overglazed with gold or silver must be free of dust and oil. To clean the piece use alcohol, which evaporates so the piece is left free of moisture.

Never let any water or dirt get onto the piece after the metallic overglaze is applied and before firing, because when fired the color will become tarnished. It is best to put the finished piece into a dust-free cabinet or container until it is ready to be fired. Also let it dry for a period of at least twenty-four hours.

After firing, if the gold or silver wears off when rubbed, it was under-fired. Gold and silver should be fired to cone 018. The best way to secure a perfect finish is to follow the basic instructions of the manufacturer for applying and firing.

BRUSHES FOR METALLICS

Never interchange brushes used for metallics. Keep separate brushes marked so one metallic does not intermix and contaminate another. Clean the brushes with alcohol. Make sure you clean them again in another clean jar of alcohol. This will ensure a proper cleansing and will keep the brushes soft. Some china paints and metallics do not mix, so you should always paint your piece with the china-paint color first, and fire, and then paint with metallic overglaze and refire a second time. In this way colors and overglazes will not be contaminated during firing.

LUSTRES

There are many lustres available at most ceramic dealers and distributors. One of the most popular is mother-of-pearl. Most of the lustres are basically the same except for the colors. There are also some now that create different designs when applied. Following directions on the jars will always give you the proper finish.

There are a few rules to remember about lustres.

1. Never let two lustres touch each other. Keep a slight space between them when applying them or they will discolor.

2. Keep lustres covered tightly when not in use. Air contaminates them. Keep out only the portion you are going to use. Leave the rest closed tight.

There is a special application used with mother-of-pearl, which I call swirling. Apply one coat to the object and let set till the coating is tacky. Then take a brush (used only for that lustre) or your fingers, which are clean, and swirl across the lustre, making spiral impressions through the area. This will give a rainbow effect when fired. You can also apply a lustre with a sponge.

Lustres can be fired at cones 017 to 020.

FIRING LUSTRES

1. Prop lid open about three inches. Turn all knobs to low.
2. After one and a half hours, turn all knobs to medium. Close the lid.
3. After another one and a half hours, turn all knobs to high. The kiln should shut off in four to five hours depending on your kiln. If not sure, follow pyrometer for temperature being reached. Follow cone and temperature schedule.

DECALS

There are many styles and manufacturers of china-paint decals. The design is imprinted on a thin film with china paint. Then it is backed with a heavier paper.

Many people feel they are cheating when they use them, but for those who are not so talented artistically, they are convenient. They are designed for your enjoyment. After you learn to china-paint well enough, you can forget decals and create your own artwork.

The decals most ceramists are familiar with are the water-mount decals. You cut out the design area to be used and soak it in water. While soaking, the decal will roll up and gradually unroll flat again. This means the decal is ready to be removed for application. It should slide off very easily, but be careful not to tear it when transferring it to the piece. Slide it off the paper backing onto the piece, then take a small rubber squeegee (which can be bought from the decal company) and lightly rub over the decal to remove any water that is underneath. Water left would cause air bubbles and marks on the decal when fired. During firing, the plastic film fires away and leaves the china-paint design.

FIRING DECALS

1. Prop the lid open about three inches. Turn all kiln knobs to low.
2. After one hour, turn all knobs to medium. If there are still fumes or smoke from film burning away, leave lid propped open.

3. After one and a half hours turn all knobs to high. By this time the lid should be ready to be closed.

Firing decals should be done according to manufacturer's cone recommendations. But usually the cone is 017 to 019, depending on the color of the decals.

CLEAR GLAZING

For those of you who prefer a high-gloss finish on your porcelain, it is very simple to achieve. They do have high-fire glazes for porcelain, but there are regular ceramic glazes that work well in the porcelain firing.

It is best to use a large flat brush to apply such a glaze, brushing it in one direction for the first coat, then in the opposite direction for the second coat. When brushing, allow the glaze to flow on.

Never glaze the porcelain until it has been bisque fired. This will ensure a perfect finish. Since porcelain is vitreous and will not soak up the liquid glaze, it will take a bit longer for it to dry. After the first coat has dried, apply the second. If the item has a number of deep crevices of detail, make sure that the glaze does not settle there, causing bubbles and possible fractures in the glaze.

When glazing near the bottom of an object, leave at least one-quarter inch margin from bottom, to allow space for the glaze to run down and cover without running down onto the floor of the kiln.

Dinnerware and plain objects that do not have much detail can be dipped. The glaze should be thinned down with water to about four parts glaze to one part water. Put the glaze into a large enough container to hold the objects being dipped. Make sure the object is held long enough after dipping for the excess glaze to run off smoothly. There will remain a light coat, which will be the glaze finish when fired.

Since the glaze is diluted you can dip the object twice. The bottom edges where the object is to rest on the kiln shelf should be dryfooted, as below.

DRYFOOTING

Dryfooting means cleaning off the glaze on the part where the item is to rest for firing in the kiln. Since porcelain cannot be placed on stilts like ceramic ware (see firing porcelain, page 146), it must rest on the base of the object. To prevent the piece from sticking to the shelf you must dryfoot the item of all glaze.

After glazing, take a sponge and lightly sponge away the glaze on the bottom of the object where it is to rest. This will prevent sticking. Make sure you have kiln-wash on the shelf as well (see page 147 for kiln-wash).

FIRING GLAZED PORCELAIN

Glaze firing need only be fired to cone 06 if using a ceramic glaze that is compatible with porcelain. Duncan clear glaze is suitable for almost all porcelain glazings.

1. Kiln lid should be propped open about three inches. Turn all knobs to low.

2. After one and a half hours turn all knobs to medium. Close lid.

3. After another one and a half hours turn all knobs to high. The kiln will shut off in about four to five hours depending on your kiln. Follow pyrometer to observe temperature and to make sure that the correct temperature is reached.

4

CREATING
YOUR
OWN
PORCELAIN
HEIRLOOMS

GINGER JAR
Hand-created violet flowers and leaves. China painted. Ronald Serfass. Jar mold by B. J. Molds.

(119)

BELTED KINGFISHER
Mold poured completely. China painted. Ronald Serfass. Mold by Trenton Mold Co.

CEDAR WAXWING AND BABY
Leaves and berries hand-created for added depth. Grassy texture also added on base. China painted. Ronald Serfass. Mold by Trenton Mold Co.

(121)

CHILDREN AND SQUIRREL
China painted. Ronald Serfass. Fired bisque by National Artcraft Co.

(122)

MUTE SWAN
Mold poured. China painted. Ronald Serfass. Mold by Holland Mold Co.

VASE WITH PANSY FLOWERS
Hand-formed flowers and leaves. China painted. Ronald Serfass. Vase mold by Duncan Mold Co.

CANADA GEESE
Mold poured. China painted. Ronald Serfass. Molds by Atlantic Mold Co.

OLD PEOPLE
Mold poured. China painted. Ronald Serfass. Molds by Schmid Mold Co.

PREPARATIONS

Heirlooms are objects that have been handed down from generation to generation. But what really makes an heirloom unique is having it made by someone you know or have known.

When deciding what you want to do, much depends upon whom you are doing it for and why. If there is something specific that a person collects or cherishes, try to create a comparable piece worthy of being left to the collector's heirs.

There are many selections of molds that can be bought for a certain creation. There are figurines, birds, animals, flowers, tea sets, dishes—literally thousands of items to pick from. If you are pouring your own wear, it would be a good idea for you to send for catalogs from the mold companies. They will be glad to send them to you. In the supply sources in the back of the book I have listed a few of the major companies with large selections to suit your tastes.

Make sure of the quality of detail of your mold. You want the creation to be your best. Some molds have ornate detail, but the overall appearance of it is smooth and not sharp.

If you really want to create a one-of-a-kind piece, or an original, incorporate different molds. The dogwood project is one specific idea that includes two different mold-piece combinations, with handmade leaves and centers. There are many different branch molds and birds that can be combined to create many original designs.

Designing the specific piece is the most important part of creating it. You can design the piece for a specific location, room, or just for a certain preference on the part of that special person. Depending on the display area available, you will have to decide how large or small the piece has to be.

Color also plays an important part; certain colors are best for certain rooms. Color combinations can usually be decided with the help of an interior decorator, if you want to really get technical.

The subject of the piece depends on what type of room it is to be displayed in. For a man's room you wouldn't want flowers or something feminine. Most likely the man would prefer animals, wildlife, or birds, depending in what direction his interests lie.

For the woman, she is apt to accept almost anything from flowers, to birds, animals, and figurines.

The following chapter contains some projects that show how to create and incorporate new ideas of your own out of different molds, paints, and porcelains. If the suggestions are followed closely you should be able to create some beautiful work. So get ready to indulge yourself. Be adventurous and try everything and anything you think would be unique. Experiment doing crazy things. If they don't work out, don't worry. You will know next time what you did wrong and how to remedy it so it does not happen again.

Some of these ideas do not have to be followed exactly. Add whatever you want if you think it will work.

NIGHT-LIGHT (USING SGRAFFITO)

For this specific night-light I used the B. J. egg mold and base.

Before pouring the egg, make sure the slip you are using is free of lumps. If it is poured and lumps occur inside the egg, when the light shines through the lumps will appear and cause spots where the porcelain is thicker.

Pour the egg shape so it is about one-quarter inch thick. This will allow easier cutting and give you more leeway for variations in thickness of the design.

You can pour the base in the same thickness. This will give it the strength to hold the weight of the egg when the piece is done.

After the greenware is poured, let it set in the mold until it is leather-hard.

The accompanying design that I drew up is for your use. Trace it onto some ceramic carbon paper, which can be bought at most ceramic shops, and then trace the impression onto the egg shape (see diagram A). If you prefer, you can draw your own design.

When cutting the design remember to use the tools that best suit the size of the area being decorated with sgraffito (see pages 51, 52, 53 for sgraffito tools, etc.).

Remember, when cutting, that you can create different depths by leaving the cuttings thicker and thinner where you want more light to shine through. But make sure you do not cut so thin that a hole comes through.

After the cutting is finished, take a wet brush and smooth out any rough edges left after cutting.

For those of you who may prefer a certain colored light, different-colored porcelain can be used. But just make sure that it has the translucency for the light to glow through.

The base on which the egg rests has to have a hole cut in the center of it where the egg rests. This hole is for the electrical parts and bulb. The bottom of the egg also must have a round hole where the egg sits.

Both holes should be cut about one-quarter inch bigger than needed, to allow for shrinkage. Otherwise, when it is fired, the hole will be too small for the addition of the light parts.

The instructions for the light parts and hookup come with any lighting kit, which can be bought at most ceramic shops.

(127)

NIGHT LAMP
Sgraffito flower work done on translucent cast egg with base. Electric light. Ronald Serfass.
Mold by B. J. Molds.

Diagram A

When firing the egg, the bottom of the egg has to be fired resting on the base. But you do not want the egg and base permanently stuck together, so you must paint the base with liquid flint. This will keep the two parts from sticking together. The purpose of keeping them apart is, if a bulb blows out you can take the egg off the base and insert a new bulb. I am sure you realize that the electrical parts are hooked up after the porcelain firing.

(129)

The firing schedule for this item is the simplified firing since there are no deep crevices and additions that need prolonged firing.

After the firing, you may if you wish add color to the flowers and leaves by china-painting, then refiring at the china-paint temperature. Just make sure, when applying the color, that you smooth the color out well because when the light shines through the streaks that are left will show (see china-painting, page 92).

This specific light was made with a plain object so the creative design could be sgraffitoed on it. But other objects can also be used as night-lights. Figures sometimes make beautiful translucent lamps. Almost any kind of object that is hollow can be made into a lamp as long as the porcelain is translucent.

VASE
(WITH WILD-ROSE HANDWORK)

The mold used for this high-necked vase is by Alberta Molds.

Make sure the slip used is free of any lumps so the opening of the neck is smooth and blemish-free.

Colored porcelain works very well for this type of object, especially the pastel blues, yellows, and pinks. I poured this vase in pastel blue, since the yellow wild rose shows up better with that background color.

Pour the vase and cast it to about a quarter-inch thickness. This will give it the strength to withhold the added flower work and leaves. If the vase is poured too thin the stress may be too great and cause the bottom to sag in.

When pouring the excess slip out of the mold, make sure the mold is sitting level so the slip runs out of the mold evenly and does not get trapped inside the mold, creating a thick casting.

Allow the vase to set in the mold until it is dry enough to take out and stand on its own, leather-hard (slightly moist). Then clean the seam lines.

After it is cleaned, put it into an airtight container or plastic bag so it does not dry out before you are ready to attach the flowers and leaves.

Cut out the petals and the leaves for the wild rose (see wild rose, pages 79, 80). There are five flowers positioned evenly around the circumference of the vase. It is best to position the flowers first, then add the leaves, and roll the vines and position them. Make sure when attaching the vines that they are moist or they will crack before you get them attached. After the vines are placed, add some buds with a small leaf on each vine.

When you attach the vines with slip, attach them only on each end of

WILD ROSE VASE
Hand-created flower work with china-painting finish. Ronald Serfass. Vase mold by Alberta's Molds.

Diagram B

the vine and in the center; and leave enough slack between each attachment so when it shrinks there will be no cracking.

The leaves are cut the same as those of the tame rose except that wild-rose leaves do not have serrated edges.

If you are brave enough by now you may want to design the positioning of the flowers yourself, but for those of you who are not, I have drawn out the arrangement I used (see diagram B). I use this design for each flower and leaf section that encircles the vase.

After all the attachments are in place, make sure there are no cracks in the vines that were added. If one appears, take a small pointed brush and paint some liquid slip over the crack, making sure the slip is the same white as the clay used.

Fire the piece at cone 7 following the prolonged-firing schedule. This is needed because the hidden areas where moisture lies must have time to dry out slowly, or there will be many cracks and splits where objects were attached.

When the kiln shuts off let the kiln cool (see firing, pages 48–50). Then prop the lid open slightly, and, when there is no heat coming out, lift the lid completely. Rushing to open the lid can cause cracking from too-rapid cooling.

Lightly sand the vase part so it is smooth. Use a 100-grit rubber scrubber. The flower work cannot very well be sanded by hand although a sand blaster does do the job. But sanding the work is not necessary.

CHINA-PAINTING
THE FLOWERS AND LEAVES

To follow the painting techniques you may want to reread about china-painting, on pages 92–111.

The colors needed for the flowers and leaves are
1. Golden Yellow Matt
2. Chestnut Brown Matt
3. Foliage Green Gloss
4. Chartreuse Gloss

Mix all the colors ahead of time so you will not have to waste time between each step in painting. And make sure the colors are oily enough so they will not dry out while you are painting.

You will need various-size shaders and stippler brushes.

The first parts you paint are the flower petals, and you use the golden yellow. With the square shader, paint the backs of all the flower petals, then take a stippler and drag the color smooth so there are no unsightly streaks. Do this to each petal around the vase.

Now paint the front side of each petal along the outer edge (see diagram 1), with the golden yellow. Then take a medium stippler and drag from the center of the flower to the outer edge, making the center of the flower a soft white (see diagram 2). Treat all flowers in this way.

Next, take some chestnut brown and paint around the stamen center (see diagram 3). Then, with a stippler, drag the brown color outward from the stamens so it blends into the yellow (see diagram 4). Make sure all the flowers are painted in basically the same depth of color.

Now take a stippler and dab it into the golden yellow and stipple over the tops of the center stamens (for stippling, see pages 96, 97). This will allow the color to get deep inside the stamen cavities.

Now lightly stipple some chestnut brown over the tops of the stamens. Then solidly cover the center berry with some chestnut brown and yellow. Paint all the flowers the same way so they look alike. After this, paint all the buds basic yellow.

Painting the leaves is the next step. Each one is done in the same way except for slight variations in the color locations. Paint with the shader brush the foliage green color under each leaf. Then the tops of the leaves are colored foliage green near the flower and the pointed ends of the leaves, chartreuse. Take a medium-size stippler and drag the colors lightly so they both blend from light green to dark. After the blending, take a pointed shader and paint a small dab of chestnut brown on the tip of each leaf. Then take a small stippler and soften the end from brown to green (see dogwood project, pages 145, 146). Do this to each leaf around the vase.

The vines are colored with the foliage green and dragged smooth with a small stippler.

After all the painting is done, make sure you clean any areas that may hold unwanted paint. This can be done with a stippler and turpentine, lightly dragging over the area to be cleaned (see page 97 for cleaning china paint).

This firing is done at cone 018.

DOGWOOD BRANCH
(MOLD INCORPORATING)

This dogwood branch is made from two different mold subjects—the branches are from one and the dogwood flowers are from another. The mold company is B. J. Molds.

Mix your porcelain slip and pour the dogwood flowers mold, leaving it cast solid. Let the pour-gate holes fill up.

When the flowers are dry enough to take out, take a pencil eraser end and press in the pour-gate hole to each flower. Push lightly and the flower should come out. If the flowers are slightly cracked it will not matter because the centers cover the joints of the flowers.

Pour the branches so they are about one-eighth to one-quarter inch thick. Then pour out the excess slip, making sure all of it has been released. If any slip remains in the mold the casting will become solid and will take longer to dry and may explode in the firing. Let the

DOGWOOD BRANCH MOLD
Incorporating hand-created leaves, branch, and flowers with china-painting finish. Ronald
Serfass. Mold by B. J. Molds.

branches set in the mold awhile to make sure they are dry enough so as
not to sag out of shape.

These leaves are the basic leaf using the gardenia leaf rubber press
forms. You will need eight leaves about two inches long. Put the leaves
on a moist paper towel or flannel in an airtight container to keep them
pliable so they can be shaped when being attached to the flower.

(135)

The branches have holes where the pour-hole gate was, and these you will want to cover up with some clay. Sponge around the holes so they are smooth. Any rough edges or jagged cuts cause splitting or cracking when high-fired in the kiln.

On both branches you will see birds' feet. Since this is a mold part of a bird piece, it has feet on it for attaching a bird. But we do not need them at this time, so clean with a cleaning tool and sponge the branches smooth. Then clean all seam lines on the branches.

Now we must cover the holes in the branches.

Brush some slip around the holes and take a small piece of clay that has been flattened and press it over the holes. Take your cleaning tool and press the clay out over the branch so it blends into the branch. After this, take a sponge and smooth out the roughness.

To join the two branches together, apply some slip on the flat area of one branch. Then take the flat end of the other branch and press them against each other. Hold them for a few seconds until you are sure they are holding fast. Then take some more slip and paint around the joint. Take some clay and press it around the joining to cover up the attachment mark. Sponge over the clay so it is smooth and blended.

The flat end part of the branch where the one bird foot was is still flat. Paint some slip over it, add a wad of clay, and smooth over it so it covers up that flat area. This will make it look like a bump in the branch.

After all attaching is completed and the branch is cleaned, turn it up.

Take the leaves that you made and apply some slip to the end of each one and press the leaves onto the branches.

Clean the edges of the dogwood flowers so they are smooth and even. Attach the dogwood flowers, applying slip to them in the center backs. Try to keep slip from dripping on the branches because you will have to clean it afterward.

Take a small amount of clay and press it through the strainer, cutting some off with your cleaning tool. Apply slip to the backs of the stamens (the sieved clay) and press onto the centers of the flowers. Using your lace tool (or needle tool) shape the center so it is evenly positioned. Do this to each flower.

Now that the whole piece is assembled, make sure that there are no cracks from drying, or drip marks that may have appeared while you worked.

The piece needs a bit of propping. The ceramic fiber should be stuffed lightly under the back of the branches where the piece extends out. And stuff some under the front flowers.

When placing the piece on the shelf for firing, make sure you have some flint spread over the shelf where the piece sits. This will keep the holes that you covered up from cracking during the firing.

These are the castings needed for the dogwood branch creation (see color section)—two branches, three flowers, and handmade leaves made with the leaf press forms.

The holes in the branches are the pour-gate holes. Sponge around the holes so they are smooth. The pour-gate hole in the lower branch has been done to compare with the unfinished one above.

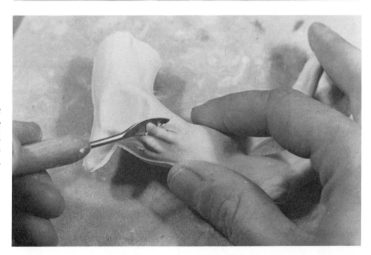

Remove the birds' feet from the branches. These are on the branches because this is a mold from another mold assemblage. Remember, this is two molds incorporated for one creation.

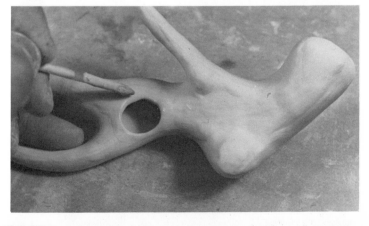

After cleaning seam lines, apply some slip around the sponged hole.

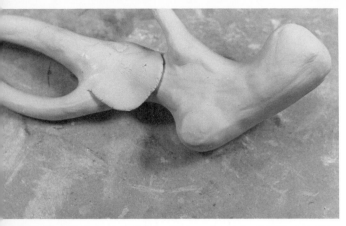

Take some moist clay and apply it over the holes on the branches. Press with your finger so the clay will stick to the slip applied.

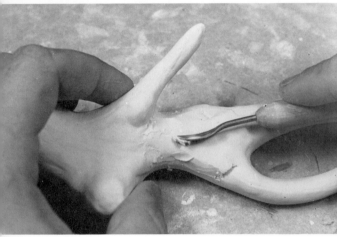

Using your cleaning tool, press the clay around the hole so the clay becomes blended into the bark of the branch.

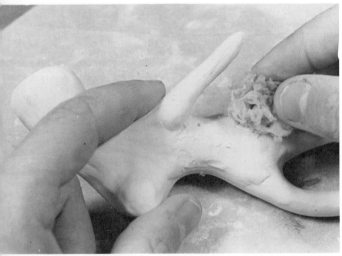

Take a moist sponge and wipe over the clay. This will smooth out any rough areas left from the cleaning tool pressing.

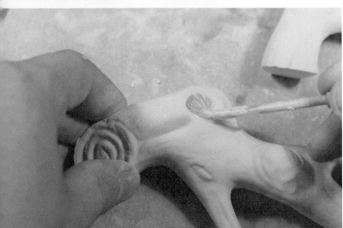

On the flat area of the branch apply some slip for the addition of the other branch.

Take the flat end of the other branch and press it onto the branch where you applied slip. Press the two areas together and hold till firmly adhered.

With a brush apply some extra slip around the joint.

Apply some moist clay over the joined area to cover up the attachment. Press the clay with a cleaning tool to fill in the groove.

On the flat area of the small branch apply a small wad of clay to make the trunk look like a stump growth on the branch.

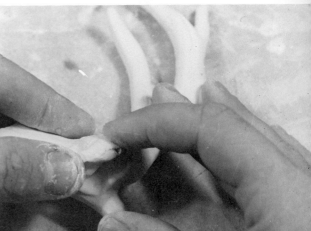

Here you can see the top bump, which was covered over with clay. Make sure it is smooth and blended into the branch.

This is how the branch assemblage should look when completed.

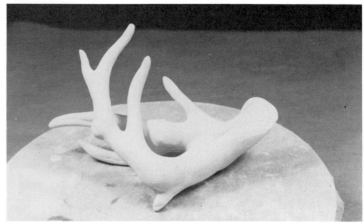

After leaves have been formed and pressed and cleaned, apply them as shown, with slip, in the locations shown here.

Apply the flowers with slip, as shown.

Press some clay through a strainer and use the sievings as the stamen centers. Apply with slip and press on with the lace tool.

The complete assembled piece.

Stuff ceramic fiber lightly underneath the back of the branch and flowers to support them so no sagging occurs in the firing.

Ceramic fiber should also be stuffed in the front of the piece so the piece does not fall forward when fired.

CHINA-PAINTING THE DOGWOOD BRANCH

The dogwood branch is a rather simple piece but when assembled and painted it becomes an elegant piece. It conveys the softness and beauty of all dogwood flowers. Very few colors are used to paint this piece. They are:

1. Chestnut Brown Matt
2. Yellow Brown Matt
3. Golden Yellow Matt
4. Grass Green Matt
5. Chartreuse

Mix all these colors separately ahead of time so you don't have to waste time between painting steps. Make sure all the colors are oily enough to stay open (wet) long enough for blending colors when needed.

Using a shader brush, apply chestnut brown over the branches, then drag with a stippler across the painted area so the color is smooth. A few streaks can add to the grain in the branch, but keep them at a minimum. If the color is applied too dark, when fired it may turn out a black brown, so keep the color a medium brown.

When dragging do not be afraid to get down in the grooves and crevices. The color that may get onto other areas can be cleaned very easily with turpentine and your stippler brush. Just drag lightly over the unwanted color and it will be removed. Then wipe clean.

Apply yellow brown to the end of the branch that is open. Drag smooth. Add chestnut brown around the circle lines and drag smooth so they blend into the yellow brown.

(142)

The backs of the leaves are colored a dark green. Apply enough color and drag with a large stippler so the color is smooth. Repeat for all the leaves.

The fronts of the leaves are painted with three colors blended together. Paint grass green under the flower area and halfway out the leaf. Then paint the other half chartreuse. Take a stippler and blend these two colors together so they blend from dark green to light green (chartreuse). Take some chestnut brown and dab a bit on the end of the leaf. Stipple that smooth so it blends into the light green.

Take some chestnut brown and paint the end of the flowers. Take a small stippler and stipple the color so it has soft edges.

Golden yellow is applied to all the centers of the flowers. Use a stippler and make sure the color gets down into all the little grooves. Take grass green and stipple across the yellow centers with this so they have a touch of green.

When completed, make sure all areas of the white flowers are pure white. The rest of the branch and flowers should be as smooth as possible. Clear up all paint accidents that may have occurred on the piece.

Fire the branch at cone 018 (china-paint firing), following the firing schedule in china-painting (page 49).

Apply the chestnut brown color all over the branches except on the open end of the branch. Smooth out any streaks or blotches with a stippler, dragging over the color.

When smoothing out the color don't hesitate to get the color on other parts of the piece. You must make sure to get the color down in the crevices so no white spots show.

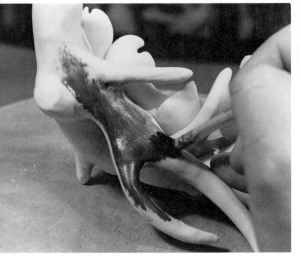

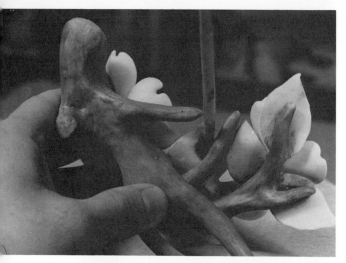

Using a large stippler brush dipped in turpentine, clean unwanted paint off the leaves and flowers.

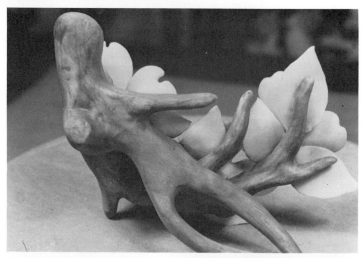

Make sure the color is as clean as you can get it. Here you can see how clean all the unpainted areas are after cleaning.

Make sure the front is spotless, especially the flowers, which should be clean porcelain white.

Apply yellow brown color to the open end of the branch. Then add some detail with the chestnut brown color. Using stipplers, smooth any roughness in the coloring.

Apply grass green to the backs of all the leaves. Then drag with a stippler to smooth out the color.

Make sure all the leaves are painted in basically the same shade. Try not to get other colors on areas that have been painted because cleaning a painted area of unwanted color is difficult after the color has dried.

The leaves on the front side are painted in grass green and chartreuse, the area close to the flower in grass green, and the end of the leaf with chartreuse.

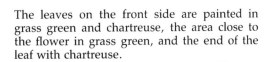

Use the stippler to blend these two colors together.

Add a small dab of chestnut brown to the end of each leaf, blending with a stippler to soften the blending from the greens to the brown.

Paint brown tips on all the leaves, making sure each leaf has the same gradation of green to brown.

Dab a small amount of chestnut brown color on the end of each flower petal and stipple golden yellow over the centers.

Using a stippler brush lightly soften the edges of the brown on the flowers so they fade into the white porcelain.

Take a small stippler and drag some grass green over the centers so they have a slight green tint. (For finished color piece, see color section.)

ELEPHANT CANDLEHOLDER (FLOWER ADDITION AND CHINA-PAINTING)

This elephant candleholder became much more interesting after a few touches were added. The mold I used was by McNees.

Since the piece was plain, I decided it needed some extra dimension, so I added a flower with leaves on both sides of the blanket. Because the blanket had a branchlike relief on it I used that as a background for the flower. The branches worked in perfectly.

After the cleaning of the seam lines, and when additions were completed, I fired it to cone 6 or 7—depending on whether you use a kiln sitter or manual shutoff (see kiln firing, pages 48, 49).

Next I chose the coloring that I wanted for the overall design. I picked poppy red, an orange shade.

The trim on the circular top and bottom was done with a light shade of the poppy red with darker line detail and triangular shapes. I used the poppy color on the blanket also, adding the dark detail and triangular shapes.

I painted the flowers in the same poppy color, with golden yellow centers. The leaves were the usual grass green, blended into the chartreuse, with chestnut brown tips, and the branches underneath the flowers were painted with chestnut brown also.

The eyes of the elephant were painted in a finishing brown gloss, to make them shiny.

After the china-painting is done, you can add some gold trim to the circular top and bottom if you like; it is a good finishing touch. You can trim the blanket, too. Just make sure the gold is applied to look dark brown (see metallics, page 112).

If you want to add a bit of shading to the elephant, since he is all white, take some robin's-egg blue color and shade lightly around his legs and ears. This will give dimension to the white.

For you who prefer your own color scheme, go right ahead. Not everyone is going to want the same coloring, and it is about time you begin making your own choices as to colors and design.

Fire the piece to cone 018 (china-paint temperature). Allow to cool properly and remove from kiln. I am sure this elephant will be quite beautiful sitting on your table beside a color-coordinated candle.

ELEPHANT CANDLEHOLDER
Added flower work and china painted. Ronald Serfass. Mold by McNees Molds
(see color section).

SONG SPARROW
WITH MORNING GLORIES

CREATING THE PIECE FOR DECORATING

If you have ever walked through any fine jewelry store or porcelain gallery, you would have noticed the unbelievable porcelain birds. Branches, flowers, and leaves surround beautifully colored birds that look so true to life you'd swear they were real.

Song Sparrow with Morning Glories is one of my favorite pieces. I created it out of mold-poured greenware, hand-pressed flowers, and cut leaves. Many hours were spent designing the first original creation. Leaves, flowers, and the bird had to be positioned correctly so that, when fired, the whole arrangement would remain intact.

Propping is an essential part of this project. Extending parts need support to hold the structure firm so it does not sag or crack in the firing.

The three casting molds needed are made by B. J. Mold Company. These are used for pouring the greenware that constitutes the framework.

Supplies needed are one gallon of white porcelain slip, a one-half-pound package of moist porcelain clay, and a small jar of plasticizer.

Tools and materials needed are a cleaning tool with curved and straight-edged ends, a No. 4 pointed shader brush, clay roller, small sponge, gardenia and violet leaf forms, a few sheets of plain white paper, and a small dish of clean water. A large-size shoe box and flannel or paper toweling will also be needed (for more information on tools, see pages 27, 162).

Cast the song sparrow's body, making sure that the slip has the consistency of light cream so when it sets up the form does not become too thick. The bird casting should be light in weight so that, when attached to the trunk, it will not be too heavy for the base. Too much weight stress will cause the base to collapse.

Since the pour hole of the bird mold is small, clean the pour gate so the hole is open enough to release the slip completely. If not, slip may get trapped inside the casting, making it very thick and heavy.

The cast pieces should all be approximately one-sixteenth to one-eighth inch thick. The base can be poured slightly thicker, to give it more strength to hold the added weight of stick-ons. The only piece that is cast solid is the leg of the bird, and this is because it is too small to cast hollow.

Make sure you clean the bottom holes of the base when cleaning out the pour gate. Sponge around the holes so they are round and smooth. Remember also to clean the greenware while still leather-hard. Keep the cast pieces in the airtight container so they stay moist till needed.

(150)

Leaves for the tree and the morning-glory vines are made with rubber press forms. The gardenia forms are used for the basic tree leaf, and the violet forms are used to press the morning-glory leaves (see page 77 for leaf making). Make sure the clay leaves are placed on a wet piece of flannel or paper towel inside the container so they stay soft and moist. This will keep them pliable, and when being attached they can be turned and shaped in different positions. Nine tree leaves of varying sizes will be needed for the branches. Eleven morning-glory leaves, in nine different sizes with two large leaves, will also be needed.

To make the morning-glory flowers, you will need the ceramic bisque press form by Trueform Flower Molds. Two molds are included in the kit, but you will use the smaller of the two. It should be free of any dirt or moisture. If you are not sure it is perfectly clean, wash it and refire it in a kiln at cone 06. This will make it like new again.

Start forming the flower by taking a medium-size pull of clay and shaping it into a flat circle (for information on clay, see pages 160–161). Make it fairly thick and at least five inches in circumference.

Lay the clay over the peak of the form, pulling it down over the shape. Wedge the clay all the way down to the bottom edge and pinch off with your fingers. The circular rim of the flower will be rough for the present.

Make sure the clay is pulled thin so the flower is delicate. If it is too thick and heavy it will lose its feeling of softness and beauty.

The clay-formed flower will dry out in a minute or so, making it possible to release it easily from the form. When the flower is separated, you can see how the peak of the form creates the deep center.

The circular rim at the top of the flower is rough and must be refined. When it has dried leather-hard, lightly sponge it with a circular motion. This will gradually make the rim perfectly smooth.

After sponging the rim of the flower, smooth the outer part where you pulled the clay over the form. Make sure this is blemish-free. Keeping all surfaces refined, you are assuring yourself of a beautifully finished piece.

Grooves and crevices formed inside the flower must also be smoothed out. Dip the small brush in the thinned-down porcelain slip and brush it over the inside of the flower, pulling the brush from the deep center to the outer rim. This will cause the slip to form a complete coating over the creases, making them disappear. Two light coats should be enough to cover all the imperfections and marks, making the morning glory an elegant, smooth-looking flower. You will need two of these done exactly the same way, making sure they are thin, clean, and smoothly finished.

Another small wad of clay is also needed to shape the flower bud. Form a thin tube of clay about three inches long. Using your fingers, twist it, making small spiral grooves so it looks as if the petals are intertwined. If you look at a morning glory bud you will understand what I mean.

Next, press out some clay and roll it thin with the clay roller. Cut a few tiny thin leaves to wrap around the bud. Attach the ends of the leaves to the base of the bud and wrap them up the sides so they surround it. Make sure the leaves are formed around the bud and not straight up and down.

After you have made the flowers and bud, put them into the airtight container, because they should stay slightly moist.

Before beginning to create the piece, make sure that all the mold-poured greenware is well cleaned and sponged, and that any lost detail is restored.

Take the base (poured greenware) and set it on a banding wheel. This will make the turning of the piece more convenient and will keep you from having to handle the piece too much. For larger pieces it is better to build on a kiln shelf that is more suitable for the size. This can also rest on the wheel, making it turnable.

Using the triangle-shaped end of your cleaning tool, cut a small hole in the parts of the trunk where the branches are to be attached. By twisting the tool in a circular motion, it will make the hole round. Wet a sponge and smooth the hole so no rough edges are left. Any roughness may cause cracking in the firing.

In order to assure good connections, put scoring marks across the two areas to be joined. This will make an interlocking joint. With your brush apply enough slip to the areas to be joined so that when they are attached and pressed together the excess slip will run out and cover the groove.

Attach the small branch on the side of the trunk, pressing against it lightly so it adheres well. Hold it a few seconds and then let it go. The remaining slip that runs out can be left to dry.

While that stick-on is drying, repeat with the larger branch on the back of the trunk. Let this excess slip also dry.

Now go back to the small branch and smooth out the area where the excessive slip is. Sponge it smooth, making sure the joint does not show. If it is still noticeable, take some clay with your tool and press it against the crevice, filling the gap. Make the clay overlap both the trunk and the branch, letting it dry for a few minutes. Now sponge it crosswise over the joint, and it should be camouflaged. Both branches should be treated the same way so no gaps are seen.

After making sure the bird is cleaned properly, brush some slip around the hole under its stomach. Make sure the hole is sponged smooth so cracking does not occur. The top flat part of the trunk should also have a small hole put into it. Sponge it and add some slip over the hole surface.

Hold the bird lightly, setting it on the trunk top. Make sure the hole on the underside of the bird is placed directly on the flat area to cover the hole. Let the slip run out from the joining so it is securely adhered. Then take a brush and smooth out any drip marks that may have run over the branch. If there are any open spaces under the bird and the trunk, fill in with more slip or clay, making sure the area is smoothed out again.

The next step must be followed closely. Before applying the leg to the bird, cut the larger end of the leg flat so it has a level area for attaching. Smooth the cut end.

Brush slip on the large area and stick it to the body. There is a slight indentation on the bird where the leg is to be joined.

After you have attached the large end, take a wet brush and apply a light coat of water over it. This softens the leg, which may have dried too much. Brushing over the leg will make it soft and workable.

Attach the thin part of the leg to the foot on the trunk. When joining it, make sure you have a slight bow in the leg so it has a little slack. This slack will keep the leg from cracking when drying. If the leg is attached tight, there will not be room for it to shrink, and it will pull and split.

With a wet brush, smooth the end part of the leg into the toe area of the foot. Apply enough slip so the joining cannot be seen. Smooth out any slip buildup.

If, before firing, you notice a crack in the leg, take a brush and dip it into the slip. Brush over the cracked area and lightly paint the slip to fill the crevice. If this is done once or twice it should cover the crack, but always smooth the surface so no harsh marks or clay buildups are seen.

Next, dab your finger in the jar of plasticizer and rub it on your palm. Take a small roll of clay and lay it on a sheet of white paper to keep the clay from sticking to the tabletop. Roll the palm over the clay, forming a thin strand, which will be used for the vines. Make sure you use enough plasticizer so the clay stays nice and moist or it will break up into pieces before you can attach it. When applying, brush slip on the ends and the center to keep cracks from occurring.

The first vine to be attached is the one on the tree. Brush a dab of slip on the end. Never apply too much slip—you will only have to clean it up afterward, and too much slip can also cause cracking.

The end of the vine is attached to the left bottom part of the tree trunk. Then it is stuck on halfway up the trunk, just above the knothole. The last point of attachment is to the small branch, letting it hang slightly over the limb. Remember to always keep slack in any slip attachment such as vines or thin areas. This vine is attached by the same procedure as that used in applying the leg. If this rule is remembered, cracking should not happen. Once in a while of course, there are things that occur in the firing that cannot be helped, but we try to keep them from happening. (Other projects using this procedure are on pages 78, 130–132.)

The vines are attached to the base in the same way. Take one vine, start at the same place as the tree vines, and slip-attach it. Lay it on the base at random with an up-and-down swirly motion. End it on the opposite side of the base. Proceed in the same way with the back vine, remembering to leave the slack between the slip joinings.

If the vines should crack anywhere, paint slip over the cracks and smooth them out again. To prevent accidents, always leave more slack than you think is needed.

Before applying the morning glories to the base vines, take your knife-edged tool and cut the bottom of the flowers so they have a flat surface. Cut them at an angle so when they are attached they can be positioned sideways. The flat surface will also make joining easier. Cutting may cause a slight hole but it will not hurt. Cut both flowers in this way.

After the bottoms are trimmed, brush some slip on the flat edge, and stick it on the location where both vines meet on the left side of the trunk. It should be tilted slightly toward the left, with its rim facing front.

Afterward, take a wet brush and smooth any slip that runs out of the joint onto the base. Then take a slip-filled brush and paint the deep inside of the flower where the hole was cut. This will fill the crack where the joining is and the hole will not show. Make sure there is sufficient slip to cover the opening.

The bud should be attached on the end of the right-side vine, on the front of the piece. Slant it slightly toward the trunk.

Next, when applying the leaves, give each one its own basic shape and curvature. To do this, the leaves should be kept moist (for further information on leaves and attaching, see pages 68, 72, 77).

The first leaves to work with are the morning-glory leaves. Always work from the left to the right side when attaching. The first leaf attached should be the first one on the left side of the base. Place it on the right side of the morning glory, where the vine joins. Press the leaf, with your cleaning tool, firmly attaching it with slip, as with all other stick-ons.

Put two small leaves on the center front flower, making sure the base of the leaf is pushed slightly down into the base of the flower. Attach one of the large leaves between the right end of the vine and the center morning glory, leaving two small leaves to be attached to the end of the vine. They should be formed around the bud, making them look as if they are growing from it.

Another large leaf is put on the back side of the base and should be placed on the left end of the vine, with a small one next to it. The other end of the vine should have a small leaf on it also.

Attach a few small pointed leaves to the two open morning glories on the lower portion where they are attached to the base. Roll out some moist clay and cut out several long and slender leaves to go around the bud. Attach them so they extend out on a curved angle. Each flower should have about three leaves.

Leaves on the tree branches are made and attached in the same way. There are four small leaves on the small branch and five on the larger branch. They can be placed where you wish as long as they are even and not all in the same area (for leaf attaching, see pages 68, 72, 77, 78).

After all leaves are attached, make sure there are no slip runs that have spread over the branches. If there are, take the wet brush or sponge and wipe them smooth.

By this time the piece has become a little drier, and you may have noticed a few more slight cracks here and there, depending on how you have attached the pieces. Fill these cracks up by brushing over them with a slip-filled brush. Make sure these patch-ups are all smooth and undetected.

After you have done your attaching as cleanly and neatly as possible and the piece is assembled, you must place it on a kiln shelf. Sprinkle flint on the shelf where the piece will be positioned, spreading it out evenly so the surface will be flat and level. The flint will keep the heat from shocking the bottom of the porcelain piece.

Lift the piece carefully and slowly from the banding wheel, setting it down on the coated area. Be careful not to jar the piece, for once it is bumped it could crumble to bits. But if everything was kept moist while it was being put together, the piece should be in good shape.

After the piece has been set on the shelf it must be propped. This is another reason that the piece should stay slightly moist, for if it gets bone dry, propping might cause it to break. Once you have begun creating the piece you must finish it and get it into the kiln before anything can happen to it.

Ceramic fiber is used for propping creations such as this (for information on propping, see pages 40, 41). Loosely stuff the cottonlike material under the extending branches and the bird's tail. Put some also under the front of the bird so there is no chance of its falling forward. When you stuff the prop, you will realize why you have to do this while the creation is still leather-hard and wet. If it were completely dry it would break almost at a touch; but you still have to be careful not to push too hard when stuffing, and stuff loosely so that when the piece shrinks, the prop has room to give. If not, the branches and tail will be pushed out of shape.

After propping, carefully lower the shelf into the kiln. Make sure there are at least four inches between the coiled walls and the piece. The red coils could also bring on a heat shock and cause the piece to explode or crack (for more information on stacking shelves, see pages

46, 47, 48). Make sure you have one-inch posts to set the shelf on so it is not sitting on the kiln floor.

Once the shelf is in the kiln, you can relax a little. There is no chance of its breaking now. The kiln will keep it from being touched until it is fired.

Another factor influencing the outcome of the creation is the firing schedule. This is a very crucial step because any abrupt surge of heat on a piece like this can cause numbers of cracks and even make the piece explode. You will probably have a slight crack here and there, but nothing such as you would have if you did not follow the proper firing schedule (for information on patching up cracks, see page 50).

The firing cone should be number 6. If the kiln has a kiln sitter (see pages 42–45 for information on kiln sitters), use a cone number 7 (for the proper firing schedule, see pages 49–50).

After the piece has been fired and taken from the kiln, use a small ceramic duster to clean away any leftover ceramic fiber. It sticks lightly to the porcelain but brushes away easily. When doing this, wear a small paint mask so as not to breathe in any of the fiber dust.

Be very careful when cleaning the fiber away not to accidentally hit the fragile leaves or vines.

After the piece is cleaned, take a grit rubber scrubber and sand down the base and the bird's body. This will make the surfaces smooth. However, the very fragile and delicate parts need not be treated this way. It would only chip and break these parts and ruin the piece.

If there are any slight cracks, they can be fixed after the painting is finished.

Now that you have brought the piece to this point, you realize there is no way you can ever duplicate each project identically. The leaves and flowers, all handmade, assure that each piece is a truly unique creation. Although the overall design is the same, the creative part makes it utterly different.

The morning glory flowers for the song sparrow piece are made with the ceramic press mold.

Take some moist clay and press out into a thin flat circular shape.

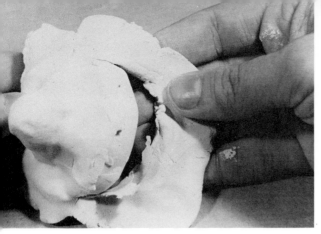

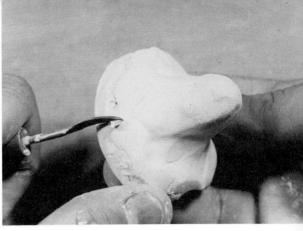

Press the clay over the flower form and pull down over the end edges, cutting off the excess clay.

With your cleaning tool cut off the excess from the end of the press mold. Try to make the cuts clean so there are no jagged edges.

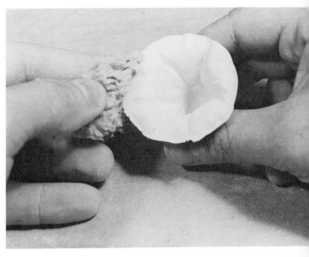

After a few minutes the clay should be hard enough to remove from form. Be careful not to pull flower out of shape.

With a moist sponge smooth out the rough edges of the flower. Here you can see the smoothed-out edge and the rough one.

After smoothing out the edges, take a brush and apply slip over the whole flower, inside and out, to cover up the cracks and crevices resulting from pressing the clay over the form. The slip will refine the flower, making it smooth and soft-looking.

For the morning glory bud, take a small tube shape of clay and twist it between your fingers to create the necessary spiral shape.

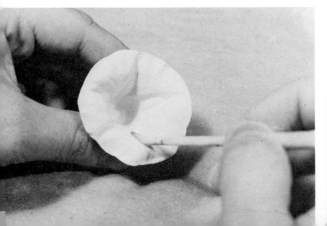

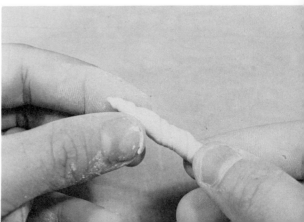

Make all the leaves for the branches and morning glory flowers and store them in a damp box until ready to use.

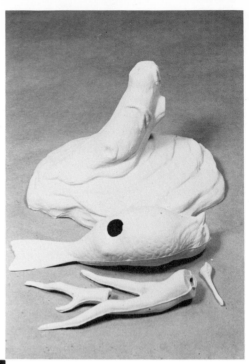

These are the cast pieces for the song sparrow creation: base and trunk, branches, bird, and leg.

Cut holes with cleaning tool into the branch areas where attachments have to be made.

Cut the hole on the under branch also.

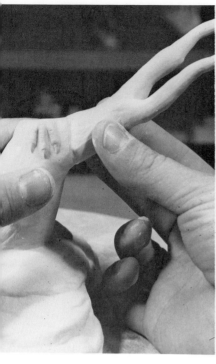

Apply slip to the flat edge next to the upper foot and attach the larger branch. Press and hold firm till adhered well.

Apply some moist clay around the joint where the branch was attached, to fill in the crevice.

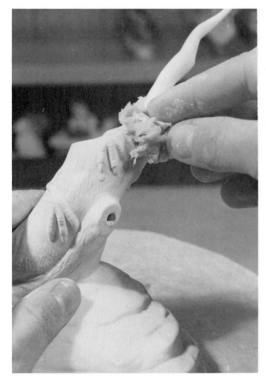

Sponge over the added clay so it is smooth and joint is not noticeable.

When completed and smoothed, the branch should look like part of the main trunk, with no joint marks visible.

Do the same with the lower branch.

Set the sparrow onto the flat surface of the top of the trunk. Attach it with slip and lightly brush around the under part of the bird so it is securely attached.

Take the leg and attach to the underside of the body. There is a slight mark where the leg is to be positioned. Press the end of the leg so it is joined to the foot on the trunk. Make sure you leave a slight bow in the leg so that when drying it has a little slack for shrinkage. Otherwise the leg may crack.

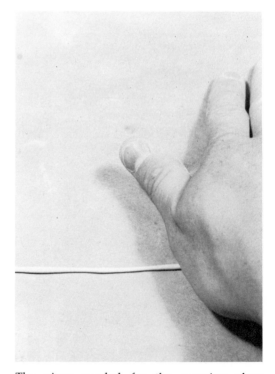

The vines needed for the morning glory flowers should not be rolled out until they are to be attached, or they will dry out and break.

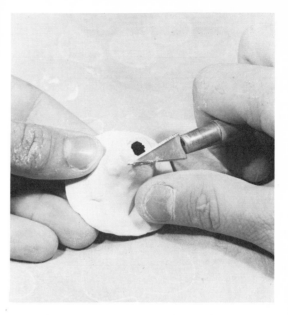

To apply the flowers, cut the back of each cone shape. This will make the attaching much simpler.

Apply the vines as shown, making sure there is enough slack between attach points. This will allow for shrinkage in drying and firing.

Paint slip on the back of the flower and attach at an angle on the end of the vine to the left of the piece. Cut small leaves and attach to the bottom area of the cone. Press firmly to make sure the leaves are secure. Do the same with the flower.

Attach both the flowers along the vines, making sure the slip is pressed into the area of attachment.

(161)

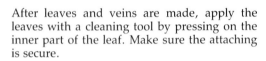

After leaves and veins are made, apply the leaves with a cleaning tool by pressing on the inner part of the leaf. Make sure the attaching is secure.

If small cracks occur when drying, apply more slip around the flower until cracking stops. Adding clay will also help if it is needed. Make sure the clay is smoothed out after applying.

Here you can see the location of the branch leaves and the flower leaves on the front of the piece.

The bud is attached on the right side of the piece with a few leaves. Wrap a few small cut leaves around the bud.

The back of the piece has a small vine with a few leaves connected to it.

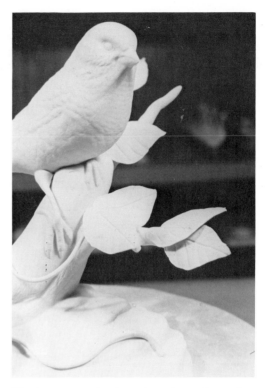

The leaves on the front branch are located as shown.

Ceramic fiber must be stuffed under the large extending branch. Make sure the stuffing is loose so that, during firing, it has leeway to push together as the piece shrinks.

Here are the leaves on the larger upper branch.

Fiber should be put underneath the bird's body to keep it from falling forward, and underneath the lower branch as well.

Stuff the back of the piece from under the branches to the tail of the bird.

DECORATING THE SONG SPARROW WITH MORNING GLORIES

The song sparrow is a remarkable piece to china-paint. The step-by-step procedures result in a very complete detailed creation.

Although the creative procedure was complicated, the china-painting is the most essential part. Without the true coloring and detail the creative part would be lost. So when following the directions and photographs, try to remember everything you have read throughout the previous chapters, and refer back to whatever you may need in order to refresh your memory.

The following colors will be needed for the overall painting of this piece. They are:

1. Yellow Brown Matt
2. Chestnut Brown Matt
3. Black Matt
4. Grass Green Matt
5. Robin's-Egg Blue Matt
6. Ebony Black Gloss
7. Finishing Brown Gloss
8. Chartreuse

(164)

The first colors to be mixed are the yellow brown, chestnut brown, black matt, and the ebony black gloss. These colors are needed for the bird.

After the bird is painted, prepare grass green, chartreuse, and robin's-egg blue, and make sure you have some more of yellow brown and chestnut brown. If not, remix some more, because all these colors will be needed for the branches, leaves, and flowers.

The following instructions can be followed along with the photographs. Remember to take your time and keep things neat. The outcome of the piece depends entirely on your patience and care.

The many steps taken throughout this project really make this creation the beautiful work of art it is. From creating the song sparrow and morning glories to the final china-painting is quite an undertaking for anyone who is just beginning to learn to work with porcelain.

If you have gone through the whole book, experimenting with the many facets of porcelain, this project when finished will have included all the information covered in the book.

This project requires pouring, cleaning, creative handwork in leaves and flowers, vines, firing up the porcelain, propping, china-painting, and the final firing.

This should be the final achievement for anyone who really wants to master this fine art. Porcelain can be used for crude sculpting, wheelwork, and abstract art, but I enjoy the finer aspects of creative porcelain. I think you will realize that porcelain has its many ifs, ands, and don'ts, but in my opinion it is still the finest art form for creating true-to-life flowers, birds, and animals.

Here you can see the painted eye. To accomplish this, completely paint the center of the eye with finishing brown gloss. Make sure the eye coverage is smooth and even. Then paint a small circle with the black gloss, making it solid in order to have a nice shiny eye when fired. When this is completely dry, take a small pointed shade brush and moisten it with some turpentine or odor-free thinner, whichever is being used. Lightly brush down the center of the eye from top to center, taking away the color. This will leave a white line, creating a highlight and dispelling the starey look.

(165)

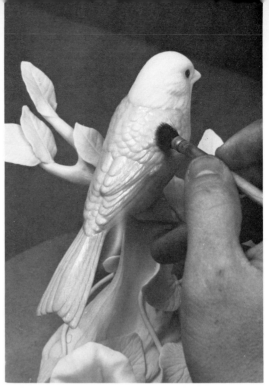

The yellow brown color should be mixed sufficiently oily to stay open (wet) long enough to be smoothed out. When you work in larger areas of color, you must keep the color wet longer in order to control it. Apply the yellow brown with a shader brush, dabbing color all over the back and tail areas. Do not apply the color too heavily or you will have to remove it where it is too thick.

With a large stippler drag over the color and smooth it out so there are no streaks or blotchy areas.

After the yellow brown is smoothed, take some chestnut brown and paint a narrow line of color around the back of the neck line. Make sure again that the color is oily enough to stay open until it is blended.

With your stippler, stipple the color to blend it gradually and evenly into the yellow brown.

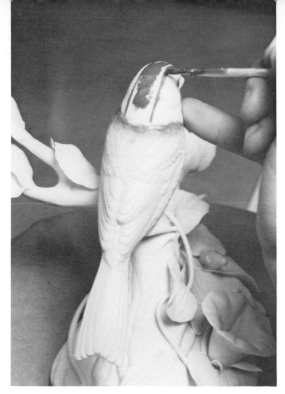

With chestnut brown, paint two lines across the top of the head, marking off the area to be covered. Fill in the whole area of the top of the head.

Take your stippler brush and drag the color smoothly over the head from the back to the front of the beak. Make sure the edges of the color are soft, the outlines delicate and softened.

Mix a small bit of matt black with some chestnut brown to make the brown color a bit darker in shade. Mix the color thoroughly with the palette knife. Using a pointed shader, paint the color around the eyes and feather it out to a point behind the eye. Leave a white area around the eye to encircle the pupil and iris.

With a medium stippler drag the color around the eyes so it is softened and smooth. Drag it out so the color feathers to the back of the eyes.

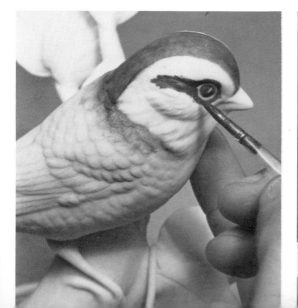

Using the same darker brown color as that around the eyes, paint a line around the beak and throat.

With a medium stippler drag over the painted line and soften the color, making sure you follow it over the beak and both sides of the head. Blend well so it is soft and feathery-looking.

The feather detail should be painted with the regular chestnut brown, using a small pointed shader. Paint this on both sides as evenly as possible. Leave the yellow brown color where the light lines are, to show the separation of the feathered wings.

This is the opposite side of the work on the head, eyes, and beak.

Take the darker mixed shade of the chestnut brown and paint darker lines under the light areas.

Here both sides have been painted. Take some dark brown mixture of color and paint the small area between wing feathers, then drag smooth with stippler.

The detail on the tail is managed with a small pointed shader. Paint the lines evenly and thin, then with a stippler drag over them so the lines are softened. The center lines on the tail are painted with a small detail brush that can create fine lines.

To add depth to the wings and feathers, paint a line of dark brown under the small side feathers.

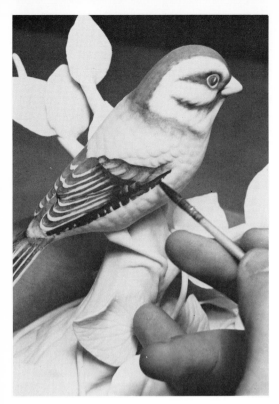

Blend the color softly, then paint the small feathers above that, dragging smooth. Next, paint a dark brown line under the wings.

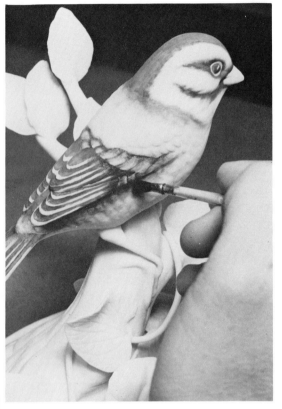

Drag the color and blend it slightly under the stomach so it softens and fades into the chest area.

Here you can see the detail work and coloring so far. Now add some matt black to the chestnut brown to make a very dark black brown. With this paint the lines on the head over the already painted chestnut brown.

Apply the same dark brown color over the back in spotted lines. Keep them even so they space out from side to side of the bird's body.

With a stippler drag over the lines so they become softened and indistinct. Blend them into the upper neck color.

Here you can see the lines on the chest. Paint them with the chestnut brown regular mix and soften them with a stippler.

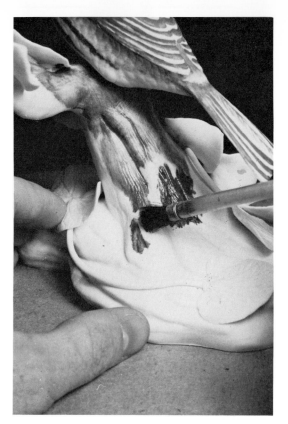

This is how your bird should look when it is completely painted. Your coloring may be slightly lighter or darker, but it should look as close to this as possible. If you are wondering about the leg, it is painted after the branch and trunk areas are finished.

Using the dark shade of chestnut brown, dab color all over the trunk and branch parts. Then, with a large stippler, drag the color, smoothing it out.

This should be the coloring of the trunk. Paint solid deep color in the grooves and crevices where depth is needed. Blend into the other color. The base is covered with yellow brown. Drag the color with a large stippler; then add the dark shade of chestnut brown in the crevices of the base for shadow and depth detail. With a stippler blend this color into the yellow brown.

The leaves on this piece are treated exactly as were the leaves on the flower vase project (see page 134). Using the grass green and chartreuse, apply the grass green to the leaf part attached to the branch and the chartreuse to the leaf's tip. Blend these two colors together.

Apply a small dab of chestnut brown to the ends of the leaves, blending it into the greens so it is soft and subtle. Here the upper leaf is blended with all three colors.

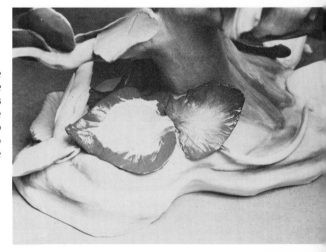

The leaves on the morning glories are treated a little differently. Paint the chartreuse color on the center of the leaves with the grass green surrounding it on the outer edges. Blend these colors together so they have light centers blending out to deeper color. Add a touch of brown to the tips if you like, blending them also.

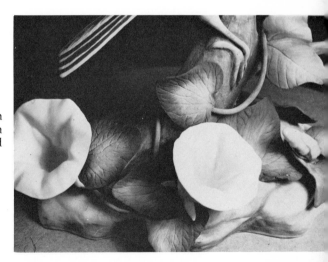

Here you can see how the leaves look when completed. The vines are painted with a half-and-half mixture of grass green and chartreuse.

Using the robin's-egg blue, dab some color down in the center of each flower. Then drag the color outward from the center to the outer edge. Paint some color around the outer edge of the circular part, then softly blend down into the center.

These are two views of the finished painted piece. The bird's feet and legs are painted last, with yellow brown. Black gloss color is applied with a pointed shader to the nails of the bird's feet. The firing is done at cone 018. Follow china-paint schedule for firing, page 49.

(175)

GLOSSARY

Absorption Soaking up of water and moisture into a porous material such as plaster.

Air bubbles Pockets of air that occur in castings after mixing of the material that was cast.

Banding The process of putting rubber bands around a mold to secure properly for casting.

Banding wheel Portable turntable for rotation of a creation while being assembled, decorated, or worked on.

Bisque Porcelain or ceramic ware that has been fired once to maturity without a glaze.

Bisque fire The first firing without a glaze.

Block mold The first mold produced off a plaster casting.

Bone ash Calcined bones used to increase opacity in the production of china.

Case mold A mold used to cast plaster molds for casting porcelain.

Casting Pouring slip into a plaster mold to produce copies or re-creations of a sculpting.

Ceramic fiber A cottonlike substance used in propping high-fired porcelain objects.

China A name given to dinnerware that has a glossy finish.

China-painted A piece of ware that has been overglazed with china paints.

China paints Powdered or premixed mineral colors which, when fired, anneal to the porcelain or glaze.

Clay A mixture of clays and other minerals to produce specific results in forming and firing.

Clay roller A tool used to roll out clay for cutting flowers and leaves.

Cleaning tool An instrument with curved and straight ends to clean seam lines and excess slip from ware.

Coils Heating elements that encircle the circumference of a kiln.

Colored porcelains White porcelain with pigment added for desired color and shades.

Cone 2 Glaze firing (high-fired).

Cone 6 and 7 Porcelain high-firing.

Cone 06 Glaze firing (low-fired).

Cone 018 China-paint and overglaze firing.

Cone (pyrometric) A three-sided pyramid composed of clay and glaze made to bend at desired temperature to shut off a kiln sitter.

Cotton lace A 100 percent cotton lace used for lace draping on figurines.

Cracking That which occurs when clay is fired too fast, or warpage when poured.

Cutters Shaped metal forms used to cut shapes for making flowers.

Damp box A container used to keep pieces damp so they will not dry out.

Decals A design printed with china paints on a plastic film which, when placed on an object and fired, is permanent.

Decorating Another word for china-painting or overglazing.

Denatured alcohol Used to clean molds so moisture does not make the mold wet. The alcohol evaporates as it cleans.

Dipping Submerging porcelain ware in glaze.

Dissection The cutting up of a sculpting to allow a three-dimensional object to be made into a mold for production.

Double cast To use two colors of porcelain to create the inside of an object in one color and the outside in another.

Dragging The motion made with a stippler brush to smooth out and blend china-paint colors.

Dried greenware Ware that has dried bone dry.

Dryfooting Cleaning off the glaze on the bottom edge of any object that must rest on a kiln shelf.

Electric kiln   The firing oven that is heated by electric coils on a 220-volt line.

Face mask   A face covering worn when using ceramic fiber for propping. It prevents breathing in of the fibers and discomfort and coughing.

Feldspar   A rock that provides the principal components of most clay bodies.

Flats   Flat non-glossy touch-up colors for touch-up corrections in china painting. Used after the china-paint firing.

Flint   A silica material used for kiln shelves so porcelain does not stick. Mixed with water it is also used to apply on areas that must touch during firing but should not be permanently attached.

Flux   A compound used in mixing with matt colors to cause them to become satin or glossy, depending on the quantity used.

Furniture   Accessories, such as shelves and posts, used inside the kiln for stacking greenware porcelain.

Gloss   Name given to china painting with a shine.

Glossies   Glossy colors to touch up incorrect colors after the china-paint firing.

Greenware   Unfired bone-dry ware.

Grit rubber scrubber   A sponge with a sandpaper substance for sanding porcelain and ceramic wares.

Hydrastone   A material that mold makers use to make the case or master mold.

Incorporating   Using molds of different mold subjects to create new ideas.

Jasperware   Name given to the style of porcelain having a dark background with white objects as the detail work.

Kaolin   Pure china clay for producing white porcelain ware. Also important in glazes.

Keys   The small circle impressions that securely lock a mold together.

Kiln   See **Electric kiln.**

Kiln wash   Substance used to coat kiln shelves where porcelain rests so the ware does not stick to shelves.

Lace draping   The art of draping porcelain-dipped lace onto figurines.

Lace tool   A tool with a fine needle end for applying dipped lace to figurines.

Leaf impression forms   Green rubber shapes used to cut and press clay leaves.

Leather-hard   Clay partially dry but still damp enough to be easily carved.

Lustre   A metallic iridescent overglaze fired at cone 018.

Manual shutoff   A kiln that has no kiln sitter to shut off the heat automatically but is manually operated.

Matt overglaze   China paints with no gloss, giving a flat finish.

Maturity The temperature at which a clay body attains maximum hardness.

Memory That which porcelain has when being fired. It remembers what happened to it before it was put into the kiln. If it was pulled out of shape and put back it will return to the out-of-shape condition.

Metallics Gold, silver, platinum, and bronze used for overglazing.

Negative impression The shape inside a mold for casting.

Odor-free thinner Another substance used instead of turpentine for mixing china paints and for cleaning brushes.

Oil of copaiba Oil that is mixed in china paint for the wetness and dryness of a color.

Overglaze China paints, metallics, lustres, and decals.

Palette A glass slab on which to grind and mix china paints.

Palette knife Tool used to grind and mix china paints.

Peephole plugs Cone-shaped objects used to close up the holes in the sides of the kilns.

Pit marks Small holes in ware caused by air bubbles and dirt.

Plaster That which is used to cast molds for casting.

Plaster cast The object made from the waste mold.

Plasticity The moisture of the clay.

Plasticizer A liquid substance used to make porcelain more plastic and pliable for forming.

Porcelain A hard translucent nonporous ware consisting mostly of kaolin, flint, and feldspar.

Posts Separators for spacing shelves throughout the kiln.

Pour-gate hole The location where the slip is poured into the mold.

Pouring bin A large porcelain holder for pouring and casting.

Press mold A ceramic bisque form on which clay is pressed to form another object.

Propping Giving an extended area support with porcelain props or ceramic fiber.

Props Either porcelain or ceramic fiber.

Pyrometer A gauge telling the temperature reached inside the kiln.

Recipe Formula for mixing porcelain.

Rubber bands Cut circular shapes used to hold molds together for pouring.

Sagging That which occurs when improper support is given to a porcelain object during firing.

Schedule Procedure for firing your kiln.

Sculpting An object created in three-dimensional form.

Sculpture Paste A water-soluble paste to fill in cracks after the china-paint firing. Flats and glossies cover the paste when it is hard and has been sanded.

Seam lines   Protruding areas of clay that appear from mold joints on greenware.

Sgraffito   The art of incising a design into a flat piece of ware, causing a recessed impression.

Shader   One of the brushes used to apply china paint.

Shelves   Flat pieces of hard firebrick on which porcelain is placed in kilns.

Shrinkage   The contraction of porcelain when fired. The piece actually shrinks in size.

Sitter   An automatic shut-off device on a kiln to shut off the heat at the desired temperature.

Slip   Liquid clay.

Sponging   Using a sponge to add texture to a smooth surface.

Stacking   Filling up the kiln with divider shelves and posts.

Stick-on   A piece of porcelain ware to be attached to a main structure or object.

Stipple   An up-and-down motion made with a stippler brush while china-painting.

Stippler   The brush used in dragging and stippling china-paint color.

Strainer   A screening material through which clay is pressed to create stamens and centers for flowers.

Student mold   A mold that is small, inexpensive, and easy to use when learning to pour. Made specifically for the beginner.

Translucency   The quality of admitting and diffusing light through porcelain objects because of their thinness.

Vitrified   When clay bodies filled with glassy silicates become sealed against moisture.

Warped mold   A mold that was unbanded or formed out of shape, causing the mold to become disfigured and unlocked.

Waste mold   The mold used to cast the plaster casting of a sculpting.

Wet greenware   Greenware that is stored in a damp box or just taken out of a mold.

SUPPLY SOURCES

KILNS

J. J. Cress Products, Inc.
1718 Floradale Avenue
South El Monte, California 91733

Duncan Kiln and Equipment
P.O. Box 7609
Fresno, California 93727

Econo Kilns
L&L Manufacturing Co.
P.O. Box 938P
Chester, Pennsylvania 19016

Even Heat Kilns
6949 Legion Road
Caseville, Michigan 48725

Paragon Kiln Industries Inc.
Dept. PC 9
Box 10133
Dallas, Texas 75207

Skutt Kilns
2618 S.E. Steele Street
Portland, Oregon 97202

Sno Industries
P.O. Box 112F
Mount Ephraim, New Jersey 08059

MOLDS

Alberta's Molds
200 East Foothill Blvd.
P.O. Box 692
Monrovia, California 91016

Atlantic Mold Co.
3660 Quakerbridge Road
Trenton, New Jersey 08619

B. J. Molds Inc.
11827 Radium
P.O. Box 32108
San Antonio, Texas 78216

Duncan Molds
P.O. Box 7827
Fresno, California 93727

Glenview Molds
2652 West Maple Avenue
Feasterville, Pennsylvania 19047

Holland Molds
1040 Pennsylvania Avenue
P.O. Box 5021
Trenton, New Jersey 08638

Jamar Mallory Studio, Inc.
6813 West Blvd.
Inglewood, California 90302

McNees Molds
P.O. Box 1386
1404 Highland Avenue
Melbourne, Florida 32935

National Artcraft Co.
23456 Mercantile Road
Commerce Park
Beachwood, Ohio 44122

Schmid Mold Co.
4054 Quakerbridge Road
Trenton, New Jersey 08619

Trenton Mold Co.
329 Whitehead Road
Trenton, New Jersey 08619

White Horse Mold Co.
3 Industrial Drive
Trenton, New Jersey 08619

FLOWER-MAKING ACCESSORIES

Kemper Tools Inc.
P.O. Box 545
Chino, California 91710

Mary Reed
Trueform Flower Molds
26 E. Edgewater Avenue
Pleasantville, New Jersey 08232

Rex Ceramic Tool and Forma Leaf
P.O. Box 29950
Columbus, Ohio 43229

PORCELAINS

Sisko Porcelain
135 Main Street
Belleville, New Jersey 07109

BRUSHES

Marx Brushes
400 Commercial Avenue
Palisades Park, New Jersey 07650

PROPPING MATERIAL (CERAMIC FIBER)

Carborundum Company
Refractories & Insulation Division
Buffalo Avenue
Niagara Falls, New York 14304

TOOLS AND ACCESSORIES

Creek Turn Ceramic Supply
Rt. 38
Hainesport, New Jersey 08036

Elsie's Ceramics of Whitehall, Inc.
331 Grape Street
Whitehall, Pennsylvania 18052

Kemper Tools Inc.
P.O. Box 545
Chino, California 91710

Staaten Ceramics
6833 Amboy Road
Staten Island, New York 10309

OVERGLAZES

Bell Ceramics
P.O. Box 127
Clermont, Florida 32711

Engelhard
Hanovia Hobby Products
1 West Central Avenue
East Newark, New Jersey 07029

L. Reusche & Company
2 Lister Avenue
Newark, New Jersey 07105

DECALS

Ceramicorner Inc.
Dept. P
P.O. Box 516
Azusa, California 91702

Coronet Decals
412 Ruth Ridge Drive
Lancaster, Pennsylvania 17601

PERIODICALS

Popular Ceramics
Los Angeles, California 90038

Ceramic World
Seattle, Washington 98109

Ceramic Arts and Crafts
Livonia, Michigan 48152

INDEX